Before He Takes You Out

The Safe Dating Guide for the 90's

Scott Lindquist

VIGAL PUBLISHERS — 1989

BEFORE HE TAKES YOU OUT
The Safe Dating Guide for the 90's

Copyright © 1989 by Scott Lindquist

All rights reserved under international and Pan-American Copyright Conventions. No part of this book may be reproduced or utilized in any form or by any means, electronic or mechanical, including photocopying, recording, or by any information storage and retrieval system, without permission in writing from the Publisher and Author.

Published in the United States by VIGAL Publishers, copyright © 1989

VIGAL Publishers
P.O. Box 71452
Marietta, Georgia 30067-1452
(404) 973-1493

BEFORE HE TAKES YOU OUT
(The Safe Dating Guide for the 90's)
LINDQUIST, SCOTT

Library of Congress Number
89 - 51783
1. ACQUAINTANCE RAPE - PREVENTION
2. DATE RAPE PREVENTION 3. DATING SAFETY
4. RAPE   INCLUDES INDEX
ISBN: 0-9623779-0-2

Cover design by: Linda Barnes
Book printed by:

MAR - LYN PRINTING
506 INDUSTRIAL DRIVE
WOODSTOCK, GA 30188
(404) 928-9413

The Safe Dating Guide for the 90's

Before he takes you out, think! What do you know about him? Does he display any of the behaviors that are listed below? The more you know about him, the more control you have and the more choices you have...do you really know him? Before he takes you out again...does he:

1. Emotionally abuse you?
2. Make decisions for you?
3. Talk negatively about women?
4. Become irrationally jealous?
5. Use a lot of drugs and alcohol?
6. Try to get you intoxicated?
7. Berate you if you don't get high with him?
8. Insist on paying your way on your dates?
9. Intimidate you by getting "too" close?
10. Touch, pinch or grab you against your will?
11. Imagine you threaten his manhood?
12. Think he's superior to you?
13. Act cruel to women, children or animals?
14. Refuse to accept a platonic relationship with you?
15. See women in "traditional" roles?
16. Have unreasonably high expectations of you?
17. Come from an abusive family?
18. Have trouble expressing his emotions?
19. Change his behavior, when he's around the guys?
20. Constantly pressure you to have sex with him?

* If you answered yes to any or all of these questions, then you need to read this book, before "he takes you out again!"

This book is dedicated to my wife, Sydney Ann Magill, without whose consistant help and support, this book would never have come to fruition. Her insight and compassion with women, as well as her efforts to help heal the victims of crime, were a constant inspiration.

Acknowledgements:

No book could come to fruition without the help and support of many other writers and authorities in the field of crime prevention and sexual assault.

In the initial stages of the writing of this book, questionnaires were sent to the major colleges and universities in the United States. I would like to commend the following people for their outstanding work in the area of rape prevention, and for their help in the research of this book.

Robert A. Staehle, Lieutenant, USF Police Dept.
University of South Florida

Laura L. Lindstadt, Police Officer, CSU Police Dept.
California State University, Chico

Mery Carol Ward, Rape Prevention Committee
North Carolina State University

Leigh Stanton, Coordinator, Women's Services
University of South Carolina

Gwen Eatherton, Director of Student Life
University of Missouri, Kansas City, Missouri

Cheryl Beil, Assistant Dean of Students
George Washington University, Washington, DC

Tom Collins, SOAR, (Students Organize Against Rape), University of Cincinnati, Cincinnati, Ohio

Kenneth Willette, Safety & Security Manager
University of Montana, Missoula, Montana

Charles J. Woodard, Vice President & Dean of Student Affairs, Savannah State College, Savannah, Georgia

Jacob Karnes, Assistant Dean of Students
University of Kentucky, Lexington, Kentucky

Jill Oliver, Counselor – Office of Dean of Students
Purdue University, Layfayette, Indiana

Diane Roberto, Coordinator – Women's Clinic
University of Connecticut, Storrs, Connecticut

Peggy Mezio, Assistant Dean of Students
University of Wisconsin, Madison, Wisconsin

Special thanks to: Mr. Ray Holloway, whose support made this work possible.

Ms. Terry Rubin, whose editorial input helped make sense of my thought and words.

Dr. Peg Ziegler, whose professional expertise and insightful contributions have made this work truly important.

Contents

Acknowlegdements — Page I

Forward — Page VII

Introduction — Page 1

Chapter One: Leaving the Nest — Page 5
Leaving home and being on your own is fun and exciting, but it can also be dangerous. Whether you're in high school, in college, or just out of the house and on your own for the first time, you need to read this book.

Chapter Two: After She Says "No," It's Rape — Page 9
Chapter Two explains the difference between rape and date rape. Can it happen to you? Who are the victims of rape? Who is the rapist? Can it be the boy next door?

Chapter Three: What Happens During a Date Rape? — Page 13
Helen's Story is a typical date rape situation that is repeated on campuses every night of the year. Her story is divided into 10 stages. Each stage is analyzed in terms of "problems and possible solutions to those problems."

Chapter Four: When and Where Does "It" Happen?   Page 25

Where are the "Danger Areas" on campus? Dorms, Fraternity Parties, Bars, Beer Parties, Off-campus housing, and isolated areas. What is Rush Week, and why is it so hazardous for young first year women students. What are the three ingredients to most date rapes, and what happens when you break the **Date Rape Triangle?**

Chapter Five: Alcohol and Drugs   Page 29

Alcohol and Drugs: the main ingredients for breaking down a woman's defenses. This chapter illustrates the importance of alcohol and drugs in a date rape. Alcohol is **not** an aphrodisiac. Alcohol dulls the senses, garbles communication, makes victims confused, and makes prosecution difficult.

Chapter Six: What Turns an Ordinary Man into a Date Rapist?   Page 39

Is there a difference between a date rapist and a stranger rapist? Why do men rape women they know? The Dating Dilemma is illustrated, as are the different ways in which men and women look at the world and approach dating. Chapter Six also takes a look at Gang Rape.

Chapter Seven: What to do if You Are Confronted   Page 51

Stage One: Communicating With Strength. Stage Two: Physical maneuvers that work/ don't work. Two maneuvers that do work, if you have the will to use them.

Chapter Eight: After the Assault, What Then? Page 63
The second struggle begins. The emotional reactions to the assault. Immediate and long-term priorities for survival.

Chapter Nine: The Medical Exam Page 73
Why do you need a medical exam after the assault? What happens during an "evidentiary exam?" This chapter takes you step by step through this important procedure, and tells you what to expect. Your rights during this process are also explained.

Chapter Ten: The Emotional Recovery Page 81
The emotional roller coaster. The most common reactions to the assault. What to expect. How your behavior may change after the rape. What are your emotional priorities? Getting your emotions under control. Your thoughts control your emotions. Listen to yourself. What is an affirmation, and how do you create one that heals? The spiritual recovery...This in **not** God's judgement.

Chapter Eleven: Man to Man Page 99
How do men justify date rape? How men can take responsibility for sexual behavior. How would it feel if they were the victim of rape? Rape, date rape, or stranger rape is a crime. Rape is not about sex, it's about power...What can a man do to stop the violence against women?

Chapter Twelve: Caring Words and Recommendations　　　　Page 109
The significant other — the common reactions to the crime. What does she need from you now? Your first instincts may not be that helpful. What can colleges and universities do?

Chapter Thirteen: Self Defense, Marital Arts, and Weapons (What Can You Do To Protect Yourself?)　　　　Page 115
What works and what doesn't work. Self defense classes — what I recommend. Using ordinary items as weapons...good idea? Common physical maneuvers. Pulling out the stops. Non-lethal weapons are the best choice.

Afterword　　　　Page 123

Fifteen Ways to Prevent Date Rape　　　　Page 125

Directory of Rape Crisis Centers　　　　Page 129
Compiled from the National Directory from the U.S. Department of Mental Health in Washington, D.C.

Bibliography of Sources and Suggested Reading　　　　Page 151

Index　　　　Page 154

Crime Prevention & Date Rape Seminar Information　　　　Page 157

FORWARD

What a pleasure to find a book that tells it like it is – the facts about dating and forced sex! Scott Lindquist strips away the confusion, guilt, "supposed to's" of our society and conveys clearly and fully, the real issues and how to handle them. He deals directly with the dynamics of sex by force and by intimidation, and most significantly he looks at the issues from the standpoint of the man on the date, as well as the woman.

"Before He Takes You Out" is readable, insightful, accurate in its analysis and suggestions even inspiring! As an eight-year dean of students and twelve-year director of a rape crisis center serving 1,000 victims yearly (including the very bright and capable who still were confused by their experience), I wish for every student, male and female, to read and discuss this book.

Peg Ziegler, Ph.D.
Director, Rape Crisis Center
Grady Memorial Hospital
Atlanta, GA 30335-3801

Dr. Ziegler is a leading psychotherapist and expert court witness in rape trauma, having supervised treatment of 14,000 survivors. She has published in medical journals, frequently appears in the media and consults across the nation, teaching medical, mental health and law enforcement professionals.

Before He Takes You Out
The Safe Dating Guide for the 90's

Introduction
"We must halt this war against women."
                                    President George Bush

Why write this book?
Because there is a need.
There is an ever-increasing amount of books, articles and related studies on the epidemic in the United States known as sexual assault. The mere mention of the word "rape" causes many women and educational institutions so much discomfort that they either ignore the problem or pretend that it doesn't exist. We can no longer honestly proclaim **"It can't happen to me!"** or **"It doesn't happen at our school!"**

The challenge facing this book is how to reach young women who are embarking on a college/university experience about the realities of date/acquaintance rape without scaring them into putting the book down. It is for this reason that I have chosen not to retell story after story of how young women are tricked and manipulated into situations where they were assaulted and raped. Instead, I have tried to simplify stories and other related crime prevention information from the most reliable and up-to-date sources into a concise "Guide to Safe Dating for the 90's."

We all know that crime is everywhere, whether we live in the urban cities, the affluent suburbs, or the uncrowded country. The criminal knows no boundaries and is more violent than at any other time in our history.

In 1988, according to the U.S. Department of Justice, 35 million people were victimized by crime in the U.S. Of that total, there were 138,000 reported rapes. That figure of 138,000 may seem low in comparison, however most experts in the criminal justice system believe that only one out of ten rapes are actually reported. This means that there were probibly 1,380,000 rapes in 1988.

We have seen a 38% increase in "reported" rapes from 1976 - 1985. This is part of a trend of 1.5 million reported rapes from 1973-82, and if we include all of the unreported rapes over that period of time, it amounts to over 15 million rapes or attempted rapes.

The "Rapist" as we have generally thought of him, is a twisted, half-crazed maniac waiting in the bushes to pounce on us. Women in general can understand the reason for caution and the necessity to take steps to prevent being attacked and assaulted by this maniac.

According to USA Today, 42% of college women don't feel safe walking alone on campus at night and statistics indicate one out of four women in college have been sexually assaulted by someone they know.

I have a beautiful four-year-old daughter named Rachael, and this book is as much for her as anyone. Perhaps when she is 17 and enters a college/university of her choice, she'll be able to go without having to worry about being manipulated and taken advantage of by so many college-age men who say they can't control themselves or that they have a right to sex, regardless of a woman's wishes.

Men must learn that **after a woman says no, it's rape.** This will take time and a lot of education from parents and schools to change the way boys think about girls, and the way men think about women. Until that happens, women will have to take a stronger stand for their rights to their own bodies. I hope this book will not just educate, but will also motivate all young girls as well as women to be more aware, awake, alert, and committed with all of their might to **not** becoming a victim.

I urge you, whether you're a high school, college, or university student, or whether you're a single woman who dates, to read this book and take action to make it a part of your pre-dating regimen, just like putting on your make-up and ironing your clothes. Take a few minutes to glance over the warning signals in this book (page 125) before you leave for that night on the town, the fraternity party, or that first or second date with the guy you just met.

The book is about **"choices."** The more choices you make at the beginning of a date, the more choices you can make at the end of the date. The more choices you have, the better your chance of getting out of a dangerous situation without being hurt.

I hope you will make the choice to read this book before something happens.

READ IT TONIGHT;

READ IT NOW!

*"Many are our joys in youth,
But oh! what happiness to live
when every hour brings
palpable access of knowledge,
when all knowledge is delight,
and sorrow is not there!*
The Prelude – 1799

Chapter One: Leaving the Nest

When you're 18 and fed up with your parents' controls, the best-looking alternative may be to get out and live your own life. It can be exciting to be on your own with no one looking over your shoulder, no one to report to, and no one telling you what to do.

Whether you're living in your own place and working at a job to pay the rent or going to college to make something of yourself, being on your own can be very exciting. Living on your own can also have its risks. Most of the time the excitement of your own place as well as the determination to "make it" without your parents' intervention can silence the real dangers of being a single woman on your own.

The euphoria of living away from home on a college campus can create a false sence of security. It is common that many young women will take risks while at school, because they feel invulnerable and protected in the college environment. This can be a dangerous, and in some cases, a fatal mistake.

Date Rape has reached epidemic proportions on our college/university campuses. Educators, school officials, security staffs, and counselors are at a loss as to how to stop date rape without saying that the university environment is unsafe. The reality is that the university is no more dangerous than any other high-density environment; however, many of us approach this community environment with little or no awareness of possible danger.

First year students are caught up with being on their own and being away from home, and tragically the thrill of that freedom supercedes any thought that crime, specifically sexual assault, can happen to them. It is especially inconceivable that a young, naive girl can be assaulted by the very guy that shares her classes with her.

Although this book is primarily concerned with "DATE" rape, it should be understood that the rapist will likely be an aquaintance of the victim. This man could be a doctor, lawyer, pastor, teacher, delivery man, salesman, brother, father, best friend or anyone that has access to the woman. Just because you don't date him doesn't mean he can't be a date/acquaintance rapist.

This is not a book about AIDS. It's a book about the other kinds of peril that unfortunately accompany the dating process. Whatever your dating habits, whether you meet that "special guy" through friends or meet him in a bar, he may not be everything you'd hoped for. Especially when you're young and in your first year in high school or college, you may want to do a lot of partying before you settle down to crack the books. You can have fun and still be careful, if you understand that a college environment is **not** as safe as your hometown. It's no different than any other small city. It has crime! It can be dangerous! You can get hurt, if you're **not** aware.

The purpose of this book is to be a **guide to safe dating.** Why does anyone need a guide to safe dating? Because even when the guy's a knockout, even when he's got everything you've ever wanted, even when everybody's telling you you're so lucky to be going out with him, "things" can happen. When you're 17, 18, 19, or 20, it's natural to think you're invulnerable. You may tend to disregard parental concern and warnings about everything from AIDS to violent crime.

You probably believe: "Date rape can never happen to me, not to me...." Right? Wrong! You are four times more likely to be raped by someone you know than a stranger, according to a recent book, titled *I Never Called It Rape,* by Robin Warshaw. Statistics taken from the largest scientific survey on the subject of Date and Acquaintance Rape indicated that 1 out of 4 women of college age has been sexually assaulted by someone she knows. That's 25%!

First year college/university women are particularly vulnerable because they may be on their own for the first time — alone on a strange campus, unfamiliar with dorm life, unaware of unsafe areas, and eager to make an impression with upper classmen. It is for this reason that they often get into situations, usually with alcohol and/or drugs, in which they are easy prey for more experienced men with little or no scruples.

Young women on their own, living in their own place and away from home, often trust men they know little or nothing about simply because the guy looks respectable and has a good job and a nice car. Meeting a man in a bar and going home with him is not only irresponsible in this day of AIDS, but is dangerous as well. You have only to remember the movie "Looking for Mr. Goodbar" to remember what can happen to you during a one night stand.

Junior and senior high school girls are also at risk for the same reasons as any other women.

Rape by a total stranger is only a small part of the over-all threat. Rape by an acquaintance or date is predominantly more likely to occur. Most of us know that we need to be careful of being attacked while walking to our cars or while shopping etc., but the greatest danger is during that "innocent" date with "Mr. Wonderful." That first, second, or third date can and often does turn into a night of terror when the woman is raped in spite of her wants, desires, and even resistance.

There are two general types of rape that will be dealt with in this book:

1. Date or Acquaintance Rape in which the victim knows the rapist. This kind of rape is different in that the victim is so unaware of what may happen to her that she often doesn't react or defend herself in the same manner as if she were being attacked by a stranger. It can be so much more devastating for a woman to be raped by her date because she trusted him. When her trust in him is destroyed, she may tend to blame herself, feel responsible, and not react in time to stop the assault before it's too late. It is estimated that only 5% of all acquaintance rapes are ever reported.

2. Stranger Rape in which the victim doesn't know the rapist. This form of rape is what most of us think of as rape. We tend to think of all rapes as a situation in which a stranger jumps out of the bushes at us. This kind of rape accounts for only 15% of all reported rapes.

You have a right .... to your own body!

You have a right .... to say NO!

You have a right .... to change your mind!

You have a right .... to NOT get raped!

You have a right .... to be believed!

> "...As long as we view rape as seduction, and at worst unwanted sex, we will never understand rape."
>
> Andrea Rechtin

Chapter Two: After She Says No, It's Rape!

Date Rape or Acquaintance Rape: What is It?

Rape is a sexual assault in which a person (usually a man) uses his penis or another object to commit vaginal, oral, or anal penetration of a victim against his or her will, by force or threats of force, or when she/he is physically and/or mentally unable to give consent.

It is important to realize that not every victim of rape has signs of physical abuse. Just because her clothes are not shredded, or her bones aren't broken, that doesn't mean she didn't resist or that she wasn't raped. The threat of force is, in many cases, just as real as the actual physical punishment for the victim. The rapist has used fear to get control from her.

Rape is a life-threatening situation.

Even though rape is a life threatening situation, the victim of a date rape may not perceive it as such. The primary difference between a stranger rape and date/acquaintance rape is the relationship between the victim and the rapist. The fact that she supposedly knows the rapist at least superficially, may make it more difficult to identify him as dangerous and this fact may also delude her friends and family into disbelieving her. Knowing him can also dilute her normal self-defense response to her attacker and cause her to hesitate in reporting the crime.

Women are four times more likely to be raped by someone they know than by a stranger.

Can it happen to you?

Yes, date rape can happen to anyone who goes out on a date or becomes involved with a man who wants sex and refuses to take no for an answer. Whether you are six or sixty or anywhere in between, date/acquaintance rape accounts for 84% of all reported rapes.

We all have a tendency to believe that it can never happen to me! We would rather not think about it or pretend that a rapist is a demented twisted freak and not the boy next door.

The boy next door?

Is it possible that the boy who is the leading quarterback for the high school football team, the son of the mayor, or the president of the senior class who is loved by everyone can also be a rapist? Yes, if the circumstances are right and he has the attitude that the girl really "wants it" and if he has never learned to take **NO** for an answer, especially if **NO** comes from a woman. Most men will disagree with this statement however, because their definition of rape or rapists do not apply to their own behavior or to themselves. Many men, as well as women, honestly believe that men can not control themselves when they are sexually turned on. They believe it is up to women to take all of the responsibility for **enticing them**. This is absolute rubbish. Whether 16 or 60, a man is perfectly able to control his sexual drive at any point, from first arousal to climax.

However, the attitude that the man is not responsible for his actions with women is not a new idea. In Arabic countries women are veiled so as not to arouse other men to infidelity. In some primitive cultures in Africa, women are physically mutilated in order to make them undesirable to men other than their husbands. And we can all remember hearing of stories of women who were forced to wear chastity belts to keep them chaste until their husbands/masters came back from the Crusades. It is unfortunate that men didn't have to wear similar contraptions, but as they were the ones in power, they were given total freedom to do anything they wished, regardless of the circumstances. Many young men still have this fantasy that they can do anything at all to a woman, regardless of her wants, desires, or needs.

I am not naive enough to believe that this book will change anybody's attitude overnight about the opposite sex. This can only be done through education, but with a little knowledge that this book has to offer, a woman may be able to recognize a dangerous man and/or situation before things get out of control.

A woman is not responsible for keeping a man in control of his own sexual responses. Each man is responsible for his own actions and no matter what a woman does, he has no right to any sexual contact with her against her will or without her knowledge.

> "...The wrongs which we seek to condemn and punish have been so calculated, so malignant and so devastating that civilization cannot tolerate their being ignored because it cannot survive their being repeated."
> Robert H. Jackson
> Opening address before the International Military Tribunal
> (1945)

Chapter Three: What Happens During a Date Rape?

The following story of one victim is symptomatic of many of the things that can happen to a woman when her date/acquaintance refuses to honor her wishes and decides to take from her what she does not want to share. Every woman's story is different but what remains is essentially the same — a breakdown in communication and a total disregard for her and her right to her own body. Helen's story may not be yours, but that doesn't mean that it can't happen to you.

Helen's story:
"I guess my story is not that unusual; many of my friends in college were also raped. We all suffered and we continue to be traumatized by what happened to us during that time. I've since learned that rape victims, like me, take longer to heal because we've had our trust taken from us. It's difficult for me to trust men. I'm always thinking: What's he got on his mind? Will he rape me when my guard's down?"

The following story is broken into ten steps that will serve to illustrate how this particular date rape progressed from innocent first contact to violence and rape.

Stage 1: Introduction and background. At this point, he may seem the perfect gentleman.

"Jim and I met during college. He was running for

student body president, and I was one of the people in his campaign. He was enormously popular, and I guess I was as impressed as every other girl was with him. I worked real hard to get him elected and after the election, he asked me out. We went to lunch, and I guess I was really impressed with him."

Stage 2: His comments and attitudes about women surface. It may become obvious at this point that he does not really respect women.

"I didn't really hear some of the things that he said. He made several remarks about women and how they tease men to get what they want and then complain when they get 'it.' I don't know why it didn't ring a bell in my head, but I guess I wasn't as much into the women's movement as I am today, so I let it pass."

Stage 3: He treats you like you're less than his equal. He makes decisions for you. He seems obsessed with control.

"A couple of days later we met for drinks in a restaurant/bar off campus. He immediately took charge of me and the whole evening. He insisted on ordering dinner for me. I was impressed with his sophistication and how the waiters catered to his commands. No wonder he was class president, he seemed born to command. He started instructing me on exactly how to eat my dinner, saying he was tired of girls who didn't know proper etiquette. I was torn between feeling pampered by his attentions and yet feeling at the same time totally ignorant, as if I had no opinion or knowledge about how to act. I realize now how all of this was only a means to control and intimidate me."

Stage 4: He plies you with alcohol and drugs — the assault begins! This is his attempt to reduce your ability to resist

"We drank for a while, and I wasn't intending to drink too much, but he kept ordering for me and insisting that

I drink up. At first I thought, why not? I didn't mind having a good time and anyway, I trusted him, God, you know, he was student body president, and every girl in the place was kind of admiring me for who I was out with. I definitely remember thinking — why's he doing this? Why does he want me to drink so much? I wasn't real sure what was going on during all this, but back then everyone in our class got drunk at least once a week anyhow, so it was probably no big deal. I don't know what happened to me after that, I think I blacked out. I was really high."

Stage 5: He manipulates you into an isolated area. The security you may be depending on (the party/gathering of friends) vanishes when you are alone with him.

Stage 6: Friends disappear. Now you are alone!

"The next thing I remember, I was in his truck and he was taking me to his place. He kept saying not to worry because there would be a lot of people there, a party of some kind, and anyway he said he'd take care of me. I didn't know at the time what he really meant. But I would soon find out. I wasn't feeling too hot at the time, drinking too much gives me a headache. I told him that I might throw up. He said I'd better not; it was a brand new truck. It didn't matter to him, he just kept driving. When we got there, I didn't see any other cars and that's the first time that voice inside me said 'Get out,' but I was so drunk that I couldn't think straight. God, I should have listened to that voice."

"He said that maybe the people had parked somewhere else, and were probably waiting for us. Somehow I knew he was lying. Why did I go in? When we got upstairs, of course there was no one there, I knew it! He was all over me from the moment we got inside the door. He said, 'You've been teasing me all evening.' He started ripping my clothes, saying, 'I gotta have it. I gotta have it.' like 'it' was something not connected to me, a thing that wasn't human. I tried to talk to him. I said, 'No, not this way, I don't want to.' He wasn't listening to me."

Stage 7: Confusion and limited escape. "What's happening to me?"

"I just couldn't believe this was happening to me. He was so popular. He was an honor student. He was student body president. This can't happen to me. Stop it, please! Let me go! I want to go home. I told him if he didn't let me go, I would be sick. He laughed and slapped me. He said that if I made a mess, I'd have to clean it up."

"When he slapped me, I knew I was in big trouble. I tried to get away from him, but I didn't know where I was. I realized I left my purse in his truck and I certainly couldn't ask him for a ride home now. I kept thinking about how I was trapped here with him and no way home."

Stage 8: He threatens you with physical violence or physically abuses you to get you to cooperate.

"I just didn't know what to do. I screamed at him that he had no right to do this. He said, 'You're all alike, all of you. You lead a man on, and then this happens. You complain and scream bloody murder that it's not what you want. It's what you wanted all along! I saw you looking at me when I was giving all those speeches. You're just playing hard to get. Well go ahead and play hard to get, cause now it's hard, and you're gonna get it!'"

Stage 9: The actual assault or rape. After the assault, he may minimize his actions or question the importance you have placed on the assault, i.e., he acts like "nothing" has happened.

"After he raped me, he acted like it was my fault. He said, 'You know, you really shouldn't turn a guy on like that. You could get hurt.' I couldn't believe what he was saying. It was like he became this father-figure, all protective and concerned about my welfare. He kept talking to me, trying to make conversation. It was like nothing happened. He actually helped me get dressed. I was so torn up inside that I was shaking. I couldn't keep from crying. He drove me home, all the way talking about me being careful and not to trust strangers around here, because it wasn't safe. I didn't say anything. I was still in shock. I went up to my room and just sat there holding myself. I remember rocking back and forth, like when I was little. He called me later that night, said that maybe we should go out next week. He actually thanked me for a wonderful night, said he'd see me tomorrow in Biology class."

Stage 10: After the assault, the symptoms may continue for many years. The most important bond, (trust) has been broken; self criticism, guilt, and self hatred may follow as the victim tries to understand what happened, and why.

"I didn't go to Biology class the next day. I left school and went home to my parents, but I couldn't tell them. I knew they wouldn't understand. My parents are good Catholics; they hardly even drink. I just couldn't take their guilt. I had enough of my own. I left school. I just couldn't go back. He was so popular, so respected by everybody, that I just thought no one would ever believe me. You know today, six years later, I still haven't told my parents. Maybe if it happened today, I wouldn't leave school, because there's more awareness about date rape. Now it seems like everyone's talking about it. I'm glad. Several years later, I talked with some of the girls that I went to school with and they said he had raped several girls and no one ever reported it. The guy's an attorney today. Some justice, huh? He's probably defending other rapists like himself!"

The following is an analysis of these stages and how Helen might have prevented herself from being raped.

Stage 1A: Introduction and background:
In this first stage, Jim appeared like the ideal man — successful, bright, an honor student, and what's even

more significant at this stage in college, he is tremendously popular.

Prevention: Helen might have found out from his former girl friends how he generally treated women.

Stage 2A: Comments and attitudes:
Many men will reveal their true feelings and attitudes about women through their off-hand comments when their guard is down. They may say disparaging things about women and their bodies. Jim made an important statement about women teasing men with their bodies and then complaining when the man gets turned on. Jim is making a common statement that many men with traditional attitudes make, that a woman is responsible for the behavior of a man. **This is a warning signal!**

He is also saying that a man will do what he wants and is justified, especially if he feels that the woman has led him on to the point of no return. Jim is also making a common statement that once a man gets turned on, he can't control himself. **This is absolutely false; of course he can control himself — he just doesn't want to.**

Prevention: Helen might have corrected him, and stated that a man is responsible for his own behavior, regardless of a woman's actions. This would have communicated to Jim that Helen is **not** like some of the more passive women that he may have gone out with. At this point Jim might have made the decision that Helen would not be an easy target and changed his mind about the assault.

Stage 3A: He treats you less than equal. He is determined to control you and make decisions for you.

Jim orders for her. He takes control of her and even makes fun of what Helen orders. Often traditional men seem to need to control their women and will go to almost any means to subdue them and/or convince their peers that their women are under their control. They may equate their ability to subjugate women with feeling in control of their own life. When they get married these kind of men may insist on control of the bank account and finances as well as insisting on making all of the major decisions in the marriage. He may also deny his wife, whom he believes to be his property, the opportunity to work, go to school, or even have friends of her own. He may be extremely jealous and publicly humiliate her in front of their friends.

Prevention: Helen could have insisted on ordering for herself. This might have communicated again to Jim that she's a woman with a "mind of her own" who cannot be controlled.

Stage 4A: He plies you with alcohol and drugs.

Jim was very obvious in his desire for Helen to not only drink, but to become intoxicated. Many men still think that the reason a woman drinks is to "loosen up." He feels he needs an advantage and alcohol is his advantage. Helen makes the statement that everyone in her class got drunk at least once a week. The most common reason for drinking in college is **not** to loosen up, but to get drunk.

Prevention: Alcohol reduces Helen's chances to prevent the crime. The more she drinks, the less control she will have. It is important to recognize what your alcohol limit is and to know the possibilities for danger when you go beyond that limit. Helen could have refused to go beyond her own limit. She could have ordered for herself, insisting that she not drink to excess or just not drink at all. **It is obvious that if you don't drink at all, you are much less likely to be taken advantage of in a date rape situation.**

Stage 5A: He manipulates you to an isolated area...the friends disappear leaving you alone with him.

This is often vital if a crime is to occur. The criminal, in most cases, must be alone with his victim without witnesses. Jim did what many men do when they're planning to rape a woman. They must have unlimited access to her without interference. Helen thought she would be safe because she was supposedly going to a party with lots of other people. She was wrong. She was tricked.

(One of the key ingredients in Ted Bundy's crimes was his need to get his victims into an isolated situation. He used various means and ways of tricking his unsuspecting victims into positions of vulnerability. Once he was alone with them, he was free to rape, torture, and kill.)

Because most date rapists do not consider forced sex a crime, they may not see the need for total isolation. In fact, he may rape you while several friends watch, as in the case of the movie "The Accused" with Jody Foster. Whereas his friends would probably stop him from torturing and killing you—they may not stop him from rape.

Prevention: Helen became trapped in an isolated area without the ability to escape or find her way home. Helen could have insisted on taking her own car or meeting Jim some place neutral and safe (some place without alcohol). Of course, after a few drinks, even if she had had her own car at the bar, she might have been unable to read the danger signals that Jim was sending and ended up in his truck anyway.

Stage 6A: Confusion and/or limited escape.

The alcohol added to Helen's confusion at this point as well as to her inability to believe what was happening to her. She had trusted Jim. He was the opposite of a traditional rapist in every sense of the word. All the reasons why he couldn't be the kind of person to rape might have flashed through her mind — honor student, student body president, and of course, he was so popular. After all, if the other students liked him so much then he can't be doing this, right? Wrong!!

Helen may have been in a state of denial at this point, which didn't change until he slapped her. Once he slapped her the reality of her situation came crashing in on her. Even though she tried to get away it was too late at this point and her options were limited.

Prevention: There weren't a lot of options open to Helen at this point. However if she had some kind of self-defense training or a non-lethal weapon that could have incapacitated Jim, she might have been able to stop him long enough to escape.

Any self defense training or martial arts takes energy and commitment to be able to use it without hesitation when and if you are confronted. Remember that just because you have taken the training, it doesn't necessarily mean you can commit to using it (hurting him). Sometimes martial arts students can function very effectively in a classroom setting but when it comes to an actual street confrontation, they may freeze. Learn to fight, not dance. (See Chapter 13: Self Defense — Model Mugging information).

Most of the date rapes that have been reported are committed with minimal to moderate acts of violence to the victim. The rapist generally depends on his physical size and weight to control his victim. I am not saying that rape is not an act of violence. I am referring to additional brutality and torture that often accompany stranger rape.

Stage 7A: He threatens you with violence to get control over you.

Jim had actually already used violence on Helen and had made it clear that he would do whatever is necessary to get what he wanted. He justified what he did and what he intended to do. For many women, the threat of violence is so shocking coming from this guy whom they trusted that they freeze and can't defend themselves. Whether the man uses physical or emotion force or intimidation on a woman, it still takes away her ability to choose. **The threat of violence is just as intimidating and paralyzing as violence itself!**

Prevention: Helen may have been able to turn the tables on Jim if she had been able to pull out all the stops and physically fight Jim rather than submit. Fighting with a date rapist is an alternative, however many women do not believe fully that a rape is happening until it is over. This is because nice guys don't rape. Right? Wrong! **Every man is a potential rapist if the situation is right, and his attitude is such that he believes he is entitled to take a woman against her will.**

Stage 8A: The rape happens and after the assault, he may minimize his actions and act like he did nothing wrong. He may even act protective and paternal towards you.

Jim did what many date rapists do after the assault; he acted conciliatory towards Helen. He helped her get dressed, acted concerned about her safety, and drove her home. He actually called her later that night to say thank you. This may seem like two separate men. But it only serves to point out the dichotomy of beliefs that many men have about women. He may act totally innocent and shocked at Helen's attitude or lack of affection for him in the following days. He doesn't understand that he's just committed rape.

Prevention: Helen could have communicated to Jim exactly what he had done and her intentions to report it to the police or to campus security. (Helen may have not wished to aggravate him after the rape by telling him she planned to report him. If the full impact of what he had done hit him, he might resort to physical violence to ensure Helen's silence.) It could be helpful for Helen's healing to express her anger at Jim. However, much of the time, the woman is in an intense state of shock and instead blames herself for what has happened instead of blaming the rapist. She may feel guilty for going out with him, for not recognizing what he was, and for not fighting hard enough against him. If she decides not to report him, she may also feel guilty for not stopping him. Her overwhelming feelings of shock, guilt, and ensuing depression may prolong her healing.

Stage 9A: After the rape, the emotional trauma may continue for many years after the crime.

For Helen the trauma lasted for years. She quit school and is affected in her relationships with men even though it has been six years later. Some psychologists have said that the trauma and broken trust lingers for many years later. If a woman is raped by a stranger in a parking lot, she can avoid parking lots and be wary of strangers. If a woman is raped by her date, her best friend, or her husband, then what does she do? She also may not be believed by friends, relatives, and authorities. Not being believed may add to her feelings of betrayal, worthlessness, guilt, and loneliness. It may cause her to bury her feelings altogether and pretend it never happened, which can cause severe damage both emotionally and physically in years to come.

Prevention: There is help. Support groups have sprung up all over the country in colleges and universities to help women deal with the trauma and to recover feelings of self worth. **Don't try to deal with it alone. Get help from women you trust — people who will believe you and not judge you. Remember, you are not alone.**

> *"The depth of darkness to which you can descend and still live is an exact measure of the height to which you can aspire to reach."*
>
> Laurens Van der Post

Chapter Four: When and Where Does it Happen?

The most dangerous time for a first year college woman occurs from move-in day to the first holiday break, for this is when rush parties happen.

Rush Week: This is a time of much excitement on campus. The fraternities are busily involved in getting new members and there are usually lots of parties, but unfortunately, where there are parties there may be lots of drugs and alcohol. Some fraternities have what they call "Little Sisters," although some greek fraternities and college administrations have now outlawed them. They are generally first year female students who help the fraternities during Rush Week. These "Little Sisters" often become "Little Victims" because they end up the prime targets for acquaintance rape and gang rape.

A first year female student is usually more vulnerable because she does not know the facts about campus life and also may not be familiar with hot spots on campus or the reputations of men who, if given the chance, will take advantage of her. She is also vulnerable because she has just left home, wants to make a good impression with the most popular guys on campus, and will probably drink to excess just to go along and be accepted.

Fraternity Parties: A fraternity can be a dangerous place for an unsuspecting woman. A frat house can be a breeding ground of hyped-up masculinity and macho. There is a strong sense of bonding and competition among the guys. Alcohol is used for one purpose and that is to get drunk. Sometimes women will be drugged without their knowledge. Her drink can be spiked even if she is only drinking Coke. A drug can be slipped into her drink when she is not looking and she may awaken later to find two or three guys raping her in the basement or an upstairs bedroom.

It must be acknowledged that some fraternities have become more sensitive to this issue and are taking a strong stand against date/acquaintance rape. I applaud their efforts!

If you go to fraternity parties, take your own means of transportation, pour your own drinks, and stay away from upstairs or basement rooms. Stay in a public place with other women. Allowing yourself to be alone with several heavily intoxicated guys can lead to gang rape.

Dorms: Dormitories should be the one place which a woman can count on for her safety, yet many acquaintance rapes occur in dorms due to the following factors. Sometimes, if it is not a coed dorm, the man or men can hide in restrooms or showers until after hours and when a woman goes to the bathroom in the middle of the night, she is then assaulted. Some women are also attacked in their rooms while they sleep. Men also gain access to private dorms because residents often leave the doors open so that they can get in after hours.

Keep your dorm door locked at all times. Never prop an exterior door open as this can allow criminal access. You may wish to carry tear gas or some other non-lethal weapon with you when you go to the restroom in the middle of the night, especially if your dorm has a reputation of allowing men in at night, or if there is a significant lack of security. (What an indictment of our society that a woman may have to carry a self defense weapon with her to the bathroom.)

Off Campus Housing, Parties, Bars, Etc.: Many date rapes occur off campus, in housing with little or no security controls or during parties where a great deal of alcohol and drugs are consumed. If a woman can be raped on campus in university-approved housing with some security measures in place, then how much more likely can it happen in an uncontrolled environment with absolutely no security or supervision?

Meeting in bars is obviously hazardous for any woman. Many men go to bars primarily to meet women, and the women they meet there are, in their opinion, available. Alcohol and bars attract what many men call bad girls and loose women. The mere fact that you are there presupposes that you are, in their minds, asking for it. Also, in the majority of date rapes, alcohol and drugs play an important part in breaking down the resistance of the woman.**You don't have to go to bed with a man. You also don't have to drink or take drugs.**

If your personal morals or code of behavior would keep you celibate and sober—don't let anyone pressure you to betray your own "inner guidance."

Deciding to go to bed with a man on the first date will in many cases spell the end of the relationship and is of course dangerously irresponsible in this age of AIDS.

Any environment or situation that isolates a woman or makes a woman dependent on one or more men for her safety and ride home can become a nightmare.

There are three factors which appear in almost every date/acquaintance rape. They are (1) Criminal Intent — the man must have the intent to commit rape, (2) Alcohol/Drugs — in many occasions, the woman becomes physically immobilized to the degree that she has consumed alcohol and/or drugs, (3) Isolation — the criminal generally must get his victim to a place where there are no witnesses.

Eventhough he may not identify himself as a criminal, the moment a man starts to assault you, he becomes one.

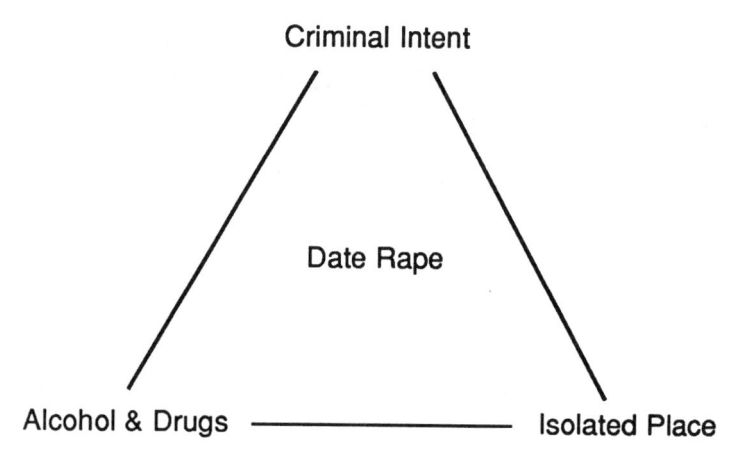

```
        Criminal Intent
           /\
          /  \
         /    \
        / Date Rape \
       /        \
      /          \
Alcohol & Drugs ——————— Isolated Place
```

Once these three factors come together, then date or acquaintance rape is a possibility. Take away any one of these and the chances of a woman being raped by her date are reduced. **Be sure you stay in an area that is either neutral or surrounded by people who are "your" friends.**

Women who don't drink and don't sleep around are obviously less likely to be caught in a rape situation, but never believe that it can't happen to you. **THE MORE MEN YOU DATE, THE MORE YOU INCREASE YOUR CHANCES OF MEETING THE DATE RAPIST. RAPE CAN AND DOES HAPPEN TO ANYONE AT ANYTIME REGARDLESS OF BEHAVIOR AND CIRCUMSTANCES.**

Think ahead! What if he is not all he said he was?

What if he tried to rape you?

What if you could not get home?

What if you could not fight back because you were too intoxicated?

What could you do to get away from him?

> *"Upon the first goblet he read this inscription: Monkey Wine; upon the second: Lion Wine; upon the third: Sheep Wine; upon the fourth: Swine Wine. These four inscriptions expressed the four descending degrees of drunkenness: the first, that which enlivens; the second, that which irritates; the third, that which stupefies; finally the last, that which brutalizes."*
>
> Ibid

Chapter Five: Alcohol and Drugs, the Main Ingredients for Breaking Down a Woman's Defenses

Remember **"Animal House"**? Beer busts, food fights, toga parties, panty raids, acting crazy, gettin' high, smokin' grass and doin' drugs. Feelin' mellow is what it's all about. When I went to college in Idaho (a small religious school), we didn't have fraternities and sororities. We couldn't drink alcohol and drugs were not even available. I can remember saying to my roommate that I missed the beer, drugs and craziness of a Berkeley or a big state school. I felt for years that something was missing in my college experience and regretted the strict religious guidelines and rules. What I think I missed more than the booze was the camaraderie and bonding that can be so enjoyable when you're 18 to 25.

Many people unfortunately still believe that alcohol and drugs can make for great times both on campus and off. However there are inherent dangers that come not only from accidents and overdoses but also from ensuing changes in a man's or woman's behavior during the dating process.

Most dates during this time of your life will include one or both of these substances unless you do not partake or if you attend a strict religious school that forbids these substances. It is important to understand what happens to people when they drink and take drugs. It is important to see and understand the relationship of alcohol and drugs to date rape.

There is a connection.

Alcohol is not an aphrodisiac. Alcohol is a depressant. Too much alcohol inhibits male sexual performance and a woman's ability to fight back.

Since many men are sexually inhibited (contrary to what they would have you believe), alcohol has gained a reputation as a sexual stimulant simply by contributing to the loss of inhibitors. However, large amounts of alcohol can have disastrous effects on sexual performance. This is why a man who is planning a date rape later in the evening will ply his date with lots of alcohol, constantly refilling her glass, but will not drink so much that he becomes drunk. He knows that if he's totally smashed he won't be able to "get it up" later that night. (Even if he is not able to have an erection, it doesn't mean he won't rape you. Rape is not about sex — it is a crime of violence. The rapist is after **power** not love.)

In the vast majority of date rape cases across the country, alcohol or drugs has been involved prior to the actual assault. It is important to understand the reason why people drink in college. It is not to relax, get high or simply to socialize. It is to get drunk. College and university students seem at times obsessed with drinking and getting drunk.

Alcohol also has a tendency to release our inhibitions and make it easier to break customs or inner laws that we normally would never do. In other words, it tends to shut down the conscience in some people and give courage to others. Ted Bundy used alcohol to increase his courage before he raped and murdered his many victims.

Recently at Boston University, the administration took measures to reduce the content of alcohol being delivered on campus by limiting the amount of alcohol permitted in dorms. Many colleges are now taking action to curb excessive alcohol consumption on campus and at school sponsored activities

Alcohol complicates the situation for a number of reasons:

1. Many men think that if you are willing to drink or take drugs with them you can't be a **"good girl."** You must therefore be the kind of girl that will also go along with sex. Many people believe that date rape only happens to "bad girls", the kind who drink, take drugs, sleep around, etc. and in fact they "ask for it." So it is the girl's fault and not the boy's. Of course those same people never fault the boys who drink, take drugs and sleep around...after all, "boys will be boys!"

2. If you go out with one or more guys and are doing your share of drinking, your senses will become dulled and clouded. In case anything happens (like a sexual assault), you are going to need all of your wits about you to be able to get out of the situation. Many times a woman is too intoxicated to understand where the rapist is taking her or even what he's going to do until it is happening to her. Once the rape has reached the advanced stages (when he is on top of you) your options are severely limited and your chances of stopping him could be impossible.

Alcohol does the following:

A. Alcohol dulls the senses.

When you go out with a guy, you will have to depend a lot on your feelings. Those unexplainable instincts that tell you at times:

"Watch out!"

"There's something wrong with him!"

"He's not treating me with respect!"

"I don't feel comfortable with him anymore!"

"I'm starting to feel afraid; I want to go home!"

"Oh my God! I think I've made a terrible mistake!"

There will be times when his behavior is not obvious enough for you to put your finger on why he makes you uncomfortable, you may have a "nagging feeling in the pit of your stomach" that something is wrong with him. In many cases where a woman has been raped or assaulted by a date or stranger, she had a feeling something was going to happen or that he was going to hurt her. She may have thought she was being silly and brushed off her inner voices with: "Oh, this is nonsense. He comes from a good family." "He's an upper-classman." "He's an honor student." "He's so good looking." "He's so popular." "I should feel honored to be out with him." She then discovers to her horror that he had every intention of raping her from the beginning. In fact, as she later learns, he has raped several other girls on campus.

The inner feeling or voice is that signal inside you that warns you that something is wrong with him or the situation. You may feel uncomfortable with him but do not know why. In many cases where a woman has been raped, she reported that she had a feeling something bad was going to happen to her but ignored her instincts and went ahead with his plans for the evening. Excessive alcohol consumption may also confuse the validity of the "inner voice" while making it difficult to take the appropriate defensive maneuvers.

B. Alcohol garbles communication:

All successful relationships are based on communication. When a relationship breaks down the most common complaint that women have is that "I can't get him to communicate."

In a dating situation, you may be out on your first date with this guy and you may have not had a lot of time to get to know him yet. You do not have time to be coy, vague, or subtle. You must be absolutely clear and precise in what you want from the date and/or what you expect from the relationship. This may seem cold and manipulative behavior, but the consequences of bad communication can be devastating.

Your words, body language and gestures are all you have to get the point across to him. Alcohol tends to garble your words and heavy drinking also affects your hearing as well as his. Have you ever noticed that when people get drunk, they tend to raise their voices? This is not only because some of their inhibitions are gone, but also because they become hard of hearing and so they tend to shout.

Before the alcohol takes effect on you or him, it is important for you to get the point across to him about whether you intend to go to bed with him or not.

1. **Speak forcefully and clearly!**
2. **Look him straight in the eyes!**
3. **Make sure he has heard you and understood you!**
4. **Make sure he understands that he and not you are responsible for his actions!**
5. **You and you alone will decide if and when you participate in any sexual activity!**
6. **Let him know, in no uncertain terms, that failure to honor your wishes will result in severe consequences for him!**
7. **Tell him "after you say no, it's rape!"**

I know this sounds extreme, especially in a dating situation, but it is better to sound strong and clear in your communication than to be silent, unclear and perceived as being weak and submissive to his will.

Understand that when you drink or do any kind of drugs, your speech becomes slurred and you may not interpret the signals that he is sending out as true warnings of an impending rape.

C. Alcohol makes you confused and disoriented.

Alcohol affects the brain. It loosens up both you and your date and it removes inhibitions. That is why so many people drink in college. Alcohol also helps people overcome rigid taboos of behavior such as: a man should never rape a woman or sexually assault her. This is the kind of rigid pattern of behavior that usually protects women from harm.

Confusion can become a major barrier to getting out of a dangerous date rape situation. You are already confused because you thought you knew this guy. You do not understand why he is doing this to you. You may not actually believe or refuse to believe what is happening to you because it is so unexpected.

Rape can happen to anyone, and yes, it can happen to you!

You may be saying to yourself that "rape only happens in cities, to other people, with strangers who jump out of bushes. Rape does not happen to college students who come from good families, who are respectable, who do not sleep around. Rapists are not good looking guys with 4.0 grade point averages. Rapists are not upperclassmen. Rapists are not fraternity brothers who are supposed to take care of you. Rape can not happen to me...can it?" Yes! Yes! Yes!

All of these pre-conceived notions are major causes of confusion during a date rape situation. Add the alcohol and now you are even more confused because you can not think straight. Alcohol also adds to your feelings of disorientation. When you are new at school, the process of orientation is stressful—new environment, new roommate, new faculty, new restrictions and rules to obey. Often when a date rape occurs, the victim is brought to a place with which she is unfamiliar. She may feel trapped and lost as to how she can get home or even get out of there. She may feel like the only way she can get home is to depend for transportation on the guy/s who are going to rape her. This feeling of being trapped is difficult enough to deal with without adding alcohol.

D. Alcohol makes you less able to defend yourself.

Alcohol saps your strength making you weaker than you normally are. To fend off a physical or sexual attack by a man or men takes a tremendous amount of strength. He is probably larger, taller, bigger and stronger than you and although most date rape situations do not involve the use of a lethal weapon by the rapist, the size, weight and strength of his body is weapon enough.

You may have to kick him, slap him, run from him or do any combination of things that could possibly deter him. You will need all your strength.

Remember he will probably not be drinking as much as you because he knows that he will need his strength to take advantage of you later. During a date rape, you have **two** enemies—the rapist and the alcohol or drugs you have consumed.

E. Alcohol makes prosecution for rape more difficult.

There are a lot of people, some of them unfortunately in the law enforcement and legal profession, who currently believe that if you drink alcohol with a guy and he ends up raping you, you asked for it. This is not true of course, but it has been a prevalent attitude; however, many people in law enforcement and the legal profesion are starting to come around. Thank God we are finally starting to change our attidude about "blaming" the victim for the rape.

Blaming the rape victim only serves to sanction rape as a justifiable form of male behavior.

Many men still believe that women "want" to be raped, perhaps not consciously, but in their subconscious. They think that a woman wants to be overpowered and subdued. It is true that some women do have fantasies about being overpowered by a strong, confident and self-assured man but this is nothing more than a subconscious desire at times to have some strong man making the decisions for her. **It is only a fantasy and it has nothing to do with the reality of a brutal rape that leaves her scarred for the rest of her life. No one in their right mind ever asks to be raped.**

In fact, during the early stages of the writing of this book, we had a few friends over for dinner and of course the discussion of date rape came up. One man's immediate concern (this is more common than you think) was "Well, what about the girl who teases a guy and gets him all turned on and then changes her mind? What about the girl who has sex with him and then the next morning decides to get even with the guy by claiming that she was raped?" This statement that men invariably bring up is, in my opinion, a learned defense mechanism against giving women power. It is also apparent that many men do not want to take any real responsibility for their own sexual behavior. For a man or anyone to say that women invent being raped to get even with a man shows how little they know of the trauma, humiliation and horror that accompanies a rape for the victim. Of course it can happen that a woman who has been repeatedly mistreated by men, may want to destroy a man's reputation by claiming rape. This is not the majority of cases—but does occasionally happen.

Rape is the only crime in which society tends to blame the victim. (This is especially true when it comes to date rape.)

It is impossible to overstate the lack of sensitivity you may get from men in law enforcement and in the courts if you have been drinking or taking drugs prior to the rape. They may simply not believe you or be willing to prosecute.

In one small town in Michigan, a college girl was raped by a date. The college believed her but a local district attorney refused to prosecute because she had one drink with him three hours earlier. The district attorney was a man.

F. Alcohol gives some men the idea that you can be manipulated and controlled if only they can get you drunk enough.

As men we have so many ideas that add to this delusion that it is no wonder we do not understand women. Remember the most romantic scene in "Gone With the Wind" where Rhett Butler has been drinking, supposedly because his wife Scarlet is in love with Ashley Wilkes. Scarlet comes downstairs to get some alcohol too. When he sees her he threatens to tear her head off to get Ashley out of her system. She rebukes him and starts for the stairs. He runs over to her, grabs her against her will and carries her up to the bedroom saying that this is one night she won't lock him out of her room. With this he carries her up the long sweeping staircase to "rape" her. The next morning Scarlet wakes up with a glowing smile on her face. Rhett, however, shows no caring or concern for her and announces that he intends to leave for London. This scene from "Gone With The Wind" also illustrates the fact that alcohol is often used by men to give them the courage to do what their conscience would normally prohibit.

Rape? I know it sounds like I just destroyed a great American classic. But the scenario is that the man in this scene raped a woman and she enjoyed it. Notice how it was alcohol that allowed Rhett Butler to overcome his inhibitions and get what he wanted. Perhaps you are saying that they were married—doesn't that make it okay? Absolutely not. **Rape is rape, no matter who does it to whom.** This kind of scenario is all too common in many films and stories. The myth is that it is okay for a man to use force to get a women into bed. She will resist a little and then she will just relax and enjoy it. There is a rampant idea on the part of men that all women want to be taken. I wonder if the shoe was on the other foot, that is if a young man was raped against his will by another man, if it would increase his awareness of the agony and horror of rape.

Although alcohol is most often prevalent during date rape situation, drugs like marijuana, cocaine and other chemicals have some of the same abilities to increase confusion and reduce a woman's ability to resist her attacker.

Unfortunately there is probably nothing that can be said in this book that will motivate a woman or a man to abstain from alcohol and drugs while going to college, but perhaps if she knows what drugs and alcohol can do to her and why the guy she is going out with is so insistent that she not only drink but drink to excess, then maybe, just maybe, she will think twice before becoming intoxicated.

"He who is bent on evil can never want occasion."
Publius Syrus
Circa 42 BC

Chapter Six: Stranger Rape/Date Rape—What Turns an Ordinary Man into a Rapist?

Although this book is an attempt to get women to be alert to the potential dangers in a dating situation, it is also a "cry in the wilderness" for men to stop their rage against women. For some people, the assumption is that if women would change their behavior, men might stop raping. That's not the case. No matter what women do, men will continue to rape until men are reeducated about women. Education, unfortunately, takes time, but until men change, women, especially young women, have to be alert, aware, and conscious that they can become a target for men's violent rage.

Why do men rape women they know? There is a slight difference in the characteristics of date rape and stranger rape.

Stranger rape is primarily an act of violence to control, humiliate and degrade the victim. The purpose of this kind of rape is to gain power through intimidation. Often sexual penetration is not completed because the turn on for the rapist is the conquest of power, not sex. This sometimes escalates into further and further acts of violence against the victim, such as the case of Ted Bundy. Stranger rape can be compared to an addict's drug habit. As his addiction increases, his need also increases for more and more drugs (or in this case, violence) to achieve the high. So do some rapists need to hurt their victim a little more with each assault until the only thing that gives them their "high" is to kill the victim.

This kind of criminal may eventually become obsessed with the thrill of killing his victim and will increase the frequency of his crime until he is caught or killed. He does not wait for the right crcumstances to commit his crime and will often go to great lengths to create the ideal situation. To this kind of criminal, age, race, sex or physical characteristics means nothing as he is not choosey.

It does not matter what you look like!

Date rape or acquaintance rape is a violent act of control perpetrated, not by a sick criminal, but by an average, ordinary guy that given the right circumstances may commit rape. He would never consider himself a rapist; indeed he would probably be offended by being compared with the run-of-the-mill rapist. The difference is that his behavior may change with the circumstances. Although it may appear as a spontaneous act, many times date rapes are not. In many cases, plans are made and people or potential witnesses are gotten rid of to make the situation safe for the rapist and unsafe for the intended victim.

There is insufficient evidence to indicate that the acquaintance rapist will eventually become the stranger rapist and one day escalate into more violent or homicidal behavior. **But when you are confronted with a man who intends to rape you, you must assume the very worst in order for you to respond with sufficient force to repel the rapist.** The man who commits date/acquaintance rape tends to be more selective in his victims and is more influenced by social standards of beauty in that his victim is someone that he would normally wish to go out with. He will often believe that he is being a man and taking a woman by force is his right. Traditional society might even agree with him.

Many of our films and media have created and continue to endorse this kind of behavior. As I mentioned earlier, "Gone With the Wind" unintentionally promoted the traditional idea that men have the right of conquest over women and, although a woman may say no and even put up a half-hearted fight, she really "wants it" and after the assault will thank the man and then reward him with her love.

Society and our courts generally would not put the acquaintance rapist in the same category as the stranger rapist; in fact the FBI does not yet include acquaintance rape as part of their sexual assault statistics. This hopefully will change as soon as the belief that somehow the woman must have caused it or is somehow responsible for the man's sexual behavior changes.

A woman is no more responsible for a man's sexual behavior than a banker is responsible for the behavior of a bank robber.

The fact is that whether a woman is raped by a stranger or by someone she knows, she has still been violated. The pain is the same, the hurt, the feeling of having her innocence stripped way is the same. In fact the trauma can be more intense when a woman is raped by her date because she had an unspoken bond of trust with him. She knows strangers are dangerous but when friends, dates, lovers or husbands become rapists, who can she trust now? Who is her enemy now?

A. The Dating Dilemma. How men and women differ in their purpose for dating.

If men and women both wanted the same things in a relationship, I am sure there would be far less miscommunication. However, this is not the case when a man is in his early years from 17 to 30, when he is preoccupied with sex. It is on his mind constantly and much of the time it is the only thing he thinks about.

A man may think that women exist for only one reason — to have sex with. This time in his life may be filled with doubts about his own masculinity, frustration, fear and a strong need to be accepted by his peers. He may feel that the only way to "prove his manhood" to himself and his peers is to force a woman into having sex.

You only have to listen to "locker room talk" to be aware of young men's unending obsession to brag about how many girls they have made it with to understand the need to prove their importance through sexual conquest.

Sex, or the ability to have sex with a woman should have nothing to do with a secure, healthy man's sense of self worth; however forced sex (rape) has a devastating effect on a woman's self worth.

Erik Johnke, a male student at Haverford College, described the subtle gender role-playing that goes on between a man and woman on a date. The following is taken from his 1987 senior thesis and from *I Never Called it Rape* by Robin Warshaw.

"The man is taught to look upon his actions on a date as a carefully constructed strategy for gaining the most territory. Every action is evaluated in terms of the final goal—intercourse. He continually pushes to see 'how far he can get.'

Every time she (his date) submits to his will, he has 'advanced' and every time she does not, he has suffered a 'retreat.' Since he already sees her as the opponent, and the date as a game or a battle, he anticipates resistance.

He knows that 'good girls don't,' and so she will probably say 'no.' But he has learned to separate himself from her and her interests. He is more concerned with winning the game. Instead of trying to communicate with her, he attempts to pressure her into saying 'yes.'

Every time she submits to his will, he sees it as a small victory (getting the date, buying her a drink, getting a kiss, or fondling her breasts). He plays upon her indecisiveness, using it as an opportunity to tell her 'what she really wants,' which is, in fact, what he wants. If her behavior is inconsistent, he tells her that she is 'fickle' or 'a tease.' If he is disinterested in her desires and believes that she is inconsistent, he is likely to ignore her even when she does express her desires directly. When she finally says, 'NO,' he simply may not listen, or he may convince himself that she is just 'playing hard to get' and that she really means 'yes.' With such a miserable failure of communication, a man can rape a woman even when she is resisting vocally and physically, and still believe that it was not rape."

A date is not a contest or a game or a battlefield. It is a chance for two people to get to know each other.

Establish your independence right away.

If you approach each dating situation on equal grounds, each having his or her own transportation, each paying his or her own expenses, then a woman is not as likely to be obligated to a man. The man is also less likely to think that she owes him sexual favors since she spent her own money. This is especially a good idea when both parties do not know each other very well.

It has been said that "a man gives love to get sex, and a woman gives sex to get love." It is obvious that men and women in many cases look for different things in dating. Of course there will always be some men who do not fit this stereotype and want more than sex from a date as well as women whose only purpose in dating is to get sex. But the difference is **a woman is not going to abuse and rape a man so that she can force him to have sex with her.** (There have been some cases of women who have raped and abused males, but this is generally a case in which the woman is much older than the male, i.e. mother and son.)

Dr. David Viscott in his recent book *I Love You, Let's Work it Out,* comments about the miscommunication about affection that often happens between men and women:

"It is especially difficult for many men to understand that the warmth and friendship of just being together is as important as sex in the relationship. Without this closeness, most women feel cheated, unloved and unwilling to be sexually involved although they may have sex in the hope that there will be a tender moment afterward.

Unfortunately, if the tender moment is not there before, it is unlikely that it will be there later.

Affection is diminished when it is misread as an invitation for sex. Mostly it is men who misinterpret affectionate approaches. The woman, usually wanting closeness with sex far removed from her mind, reaches out to be affectionate to her mate and finds him suddenly aroused, thinking she wants to make love. This disappoints and hurts her and she pulls back. He accuses her of starting something she won't finish."

It is at this point, that the man, if he's aggressive and determined, and if he feels that his manhood has been abused, may use force to finish what he thinks the woman started in the first place.

It is in this kind of situation that he feels totally justified to take from a woman what she does not want to give. He certainly does not interpret his actions as rape.

From *I Never Called it Rape* by Robin Warshaw:
"Some acquaintance rapists become oddly tender immediately afterward and try to dress the woman or cover them. Some gallantly insist on walking or driving their victims home, telling the woman that it's dangerous for them to be out alone. Others profess love and talk about having an ongoing relationship. Another type kisses their victims good-by and says they will call them again soon. (And some do call, apparently raring to go on another "date.") In short, many men fail to perceive that what has just happened was RAPE."

B. If a man wants sex, why doesn't he just ask?

Why do so many men find it necessary to manipulate and control their women for sexual gratification?

Women:
When a woman wants sex from a man, she will generally communicate her desires by subtle or direct means. Rarely do you hear of a woman getting a guy drunk, plying him with drugs or forcing herself on him.

The reasons for this behavior or lack of behavior go beyond the fact that her size may prevent her from forcing him to have sex. There are also other reasons. Most women are used to communicating their desires to others and generally do not seem to have the need for physical power over another individual to feel good about themselves. They are also used to dealing with rejection if he says no. In addition, many women are conditioned since childhood not to be aggressive about sex. They are taught to be submissive and wait for the man's lead.

Men:
Many men are so unaccustomed to handling rejection that they can not bring themselves to openly ask a woman for sex. This would give her too much power and she could say no. Therefore, he may think he needs to reduce her ability to think and resist by giving her alcohol and drugs. He needs to make her weaker and more passive than she normally is so that he can "have his way" with her.

Gang Rape:
Some men feel so inferior to women that they can't "do it" alone. I am referring to **gang rape**. This is sometimes called "gang-bang," or "trains" which is a college or fraternity slang expression for gang rapes, so called because the men line up like cars on a train. Each man, like a railroad car, takes his turn raping the girl.

In *Against Our Will,* Susan Brownmiller writes: *"When men rape in pairs or gangs, the sheer physical advantage of their position is clear-cut and unquestionable. No simple conquest of men over woman."*

Gang bang is not group sex!!!
Gang bang often turns into gang rape and often becomes the most brutal, violent abuse of a woman's body imaginable.

Robin Warsaw, in *I Never Called it Rape,* also states that *"men who rape in groups might never commit rape alone. When men participate in gang rape, they bond with their group, and they reduce their victim to nothing more than a collective vessel for their 'masculinity.' Through their rape, they also prove their sexual ability to the group, and underscore their status. Often the group leader is the first man to rape the woman; his underlings then follow. Gang bang is not group sex. the concept of one woman and many men is so diametrically opposed to equality and consent that violence often escalates. The woman is so debased in this situation that insult, forced fellatio, pulling, biting and burning the breasts, urinating on the victim, smearing semen on the victim is part of the act. The level of violence also tends to increase as each man takes his turn."*

A woman's needs and desires for tenderness and caring in a sexual relationship will be totally destroyed in a gang bang/rape. The gang rape is so much more violent and devastating to not only a woman's body, but also to her dignity and self worth that it can cause irreparable psychic harm. Gang rape is the ultimate destruction of women by men.

C. Where does it all start?

Date rape does not start with the actual assault, but with the formative stages in our lives when boys and girls learn to look at the world differently. To understand these differences in the way a man approaches life as compared to a woman's approach, we need to turn to *New Life for Men* by Joe Vaughn and Ron Klug.

"The beaten path for men is a way of life dominated by an excessive need to control oneself, one's environment, and others. The male emphasis on independence and assertiveness does not encourage the admission of inadequacy, fear, or personal uncertainty. Typically 'masculine' traits like competitiveness, self reliance, and toughness are not wrong or bad. **They become harmful**

only when they are pursued to the exclusion of others."

Vaughn and Klug also state that in talking with a number of men, they discovered that the feelings that seem to trouble men most were anger, sexual attraction to women, and fear—particularly fear of failure...Those (men) who are threatened by their own strong feelings of inadequacy and personal insecurity have a desperate need to deny feelings, because these emotions seem to prove the already negative judgement they have handed down on their own masculinity.

To admit to having feelings would be to acknowledge that they are not "real men."

These men often:
1. Refuse to handle their feelings
2. Need to be in charge.
3. Need to dominate conversations.
4. Brag about their successes.
5. Maintain that they have no weaknesses.

During a crisis, a man:
1. May frequently not be there physically or emotionally.
2. May be surprised when women get upset. He may not understand or fathom what you are feeling, since he is not used to expressing his own feelings.
3. May tend to minimize the importance you place on events. This minimizing is his way of devaluing women in general and you in particular.

4. May not not listen to your opinions and even if he does, he may ignore you and do what he wants anyway, regardless of your feelings.

The male vs. female attitude:

The following is an overview of attitudes, common belief systems, and behaviors. There are exceptions.

Male		Female
1. Competitive	vs.	Cooperative
2. Performance	vs.	Participation
3. Dominance	vs.	Equality
4. Power	vs.	Share power
5. Suppress emotions	vs.	Express emotions
6. Skepticism	vs.	Trust others
7. Neglect other's needs	vs.	Awareness of other's needs
8. Judge others	vs.	Accept others
9. Self acceptance	vs.	Self judgement
10. Control others	vs.	Feels out of control

Is it any wonder, when we look at the basic differences in the way men and women view the world, that inequality and conflict are bound to occur? In general men are "outer directed" whereas women are "inner directed." When a man is fired from a job, he will often blame his boss, society, the company or anything he can think of that is outside of himself. When problems occur, he gets more active, works harder and rarely takes the time to analyze himself to find the problem. This may account for the fact that when a woman is not responding to his sexual advances, instead of questioning his actions, her needs, the place, time or appropriateness of having sex at all, he steam-rolls ahead with more determination than before.

He is action oriented and believes that success comes with more effort. It is reported that Donald Trump's parting words to all of his staff is "Push Harder!" I'm sure that Mr. Trump would be the first to qualify his remarks to business and achievement. However, is it any wonder that when a man is used to solving all of his problems with this kind of solution, it would be unlikely for him to try another more sensitive and considerate approach, even when his objective is a human one.

Women tend to communicate by talking out their problems. They also tend to look within themselves or find a supportive friend or group to solve personal problems. They question, search, probe and analyze themselves to find answers. If a woman is fired, she may try to figure out what she did wrong or how she caused it; however, she may be too critical of herself. As long as a woman thinks she has to bend over backwards to be acceptable to a man or to feel good about herself then her self worth will depend, not on pleasing herself, but men. This totally false concept of self leads many women to constantly question their self worth and blame themselves for being raped. They may wonder why they agreed to go out with the "jerk," didn't fight back, drank too much, etc. They often forget who did the raping. They may blame themselves instead of the rapist.

The recent *Ms.* magazine survey on date rape as reported in "I Never Called it Rape," by Robin Warshaw states: *"41% of the raped women who had been raped by an acquaintance expected to be raped again."* This attitude may keep them in a victim role instead of making the transfer to an attitude of a **survivor.**

Victims who identify themselves as victims often become victims again and again, those who think of themselves as survivors have a much better chance of making it through the ordeal.

Survivors tend to get help, get involved and get on with their life. It's all in the attitude. No matter what happened, you did nothing that made you deserving of rape. Remember who committed the crime! Keep saying:
    I will survive this.
    I am a survivor.
    I will not be a victim again.
    I will make it through this.
The most significant factor in identifying yourself as a survivor and not a helpless victim is getting help.

> *"...Though I walk through the valley of the shadow of death, I will fear no evil: for thou art with me; Thy rod and thy staff they comfort me."*
> The 23rd Psalm

Chapter Seven: What to do if You Are Confronted.

Whatever differences there may be in background, purpose, education or self worth between a stranger rapist and an acquaintance rapist, those differences disappear at the moment of the assault. Once the rapist makes his move, the outcome for the woman is always the same: pain, horror, trauma and shock.

Naturally it is important to practice as much prevention as possible and that includes moderation of alcohol and watching of signs that he may be giving off. **There are no guarantees that rape will not happen to you no matter how careful you are and no matter how well prepared you are.** There are only alternatives for behavior that, if taken, might prevent the situation from getting out of control. **Remember: the more choices you make in the beginning of the evening, the more options you tend to have at the end of the evening.**

Rape is an act of violence and control, not an act of sex, love or seduction. Even if you lose control in a dating situation, you can regain what youve lost by re-establishing a strong line of direct communication.

Stage I: Communicating With Strength

First of all, try to talk to him. Be clear in your communication. The earlier your wishes are known to him, the more likely he will honor your desires or lack of desires for him. As the evening goes on, he may either not believe you or think you are playing hard to get.

Remember, your words are only 7% of your communication, 38% is the tone of your voice, and 55% of your communication is non-verbal. In other words, your tone of voice and your body language must match your words.

How can I hear what you say, when your actions are thundering in my ears!

Your communication carries more weight if you make your feelings clear to him at the start.

You can achieve success if you can get him to:
a. Stop the momentum long enough for him to look at you.
b. Get him to think about what he is doing.
c. Get him to think about the negative consequences of his actions.
d. Get him to think about you as a person, not as some "thing" he has the right to conquer.

* All of the following statements should only be used in a date or acquaintance rape situation — they may not be successful if he is a stranger.

Here are some possibilities that you might try. Remember that he may not be listening to you so you need to communicate with strength and clarity. Make your statements strong. You may try to lower your voice a little as a high voice can sound weak and too feminine for him to take you seriously. He may tend to listen to you more if your voice is harder and stronger.

The following statements are suggestions that may work for you. There is no one statement or group of words that will work in all situations. Every situation is different. **Use your instincts. Listen to that inner voice and let it guide you on how you can best reach this guy.** You must do it **now,** before he becomes unreachable by your words.

Early in the evening (before things get physical):

1. "I want you to know that I'm not interested in a physical relationship right now and I would appreciate it if you would not pressure me at this point and honor my feelings. Okay?"
2. "I would feel more comfortable if we met each other at the _____ (a neutral territory). Okay?"
3. "I want to drive my car as I feel safer that way. Please understand, this is no reflection on you. This is something I always do during the first few dates. Okay?"
4. "I don't appreciate your statement about women. I am a woman too and when you talk about women, you are talking about me. If you want my respect, you must show me that you respect not only me, but all women as well!"
5. "Is that a put down? If it is, I don't appreciate it. Please don't do that again. Okay?"
  (Do not be afraid to pin him down for his comments. If you sit there and take it or say nothing, he may either assume that you agree with him or are too weak to confront him and that you will also say nothing later if and when he begins to rape you.)
6. "I'm feeling uncomfortable with your behavior. I want to go home. Please take me home. Right Now."
  (If you are uncomfortable with his behavior or the way the evening is turning out, you may want to have an available friend who can come and pick you up.)
7. "I'm going home. You don't have to drive me; I have my own car."
8. "I don't feel like drinking. Please don't pressure me to drink when I don't want to."
  (You may indicate to him that you are not going to drink by turning your glass over or by telling the server that you will not be drinking tonight so that

they can take the wine glass away. Involving the server is a good idea because you now have a witness that you did not drink or stopped drinking at some point in the evening. This person could be called upon in a trial situation to attest to the fact that you were not intoxicated during this portion of the date.)

You will notice that in statements 1 - 5, each statement is followed by an Okay?. There is a good reason for this. You are asking for his acknowledgement and agreement with your desires and wishes. **You are *not* asking for his permission.** You also want to know if he has heard you. Men often turn women off in their head and do not really listen to their words. This is not necessarily done with malice or even consciously, but often they are not used to listening to women and are self absorbed. **You must be sure that your communication has been heard and understood.** Later in the evening, if his behavior is in conflict with his earlier agreement with your wishes, he can be reminded of his agreement.

As he starts to get more physical with you:
(These are only suggestions; put them into your own words if necessary.)

9. "Back off! I need my space!"

10. "Stop touching me! I don't want you to do that! Stop it now!"

11. "What you are doing is making me uncomfortable. Please stop it **right now!**"

12. "What do you think you're doing?"

13. "Are you trying to get me drunk so that you can take advantage of me?"
    (This is no joke, so do not let him humor or patronize you by not taking you seriously.)

14. "Why are you trying to get me drunk? Remember our agreement—that I'm **not** going to bed with you tonight!"

In the first stages of the assault:

15.. "I know what you're trying to do. It's called **rape!**"

16. "I want you to know that I know what you are trying to do and if you continue, I will report you to campus security **and** the police department."

17. "Are you prepared for the consequences of your actions?"

18. "Are you prepared to be branded a 'Rapist' by me and the police?"

19. "Are you prepared for what will happen to you if you continue this assault?

   a. You will lose your standing at the University.

   b. You will be known as a rapist.

   c. You will not be able to get a decent job and there is every possibility that you will go to jail!

   d. Are you prepared for that? If so, then I'm warning you that I will fight you with all of my strength!

   e. I will prosecute you to the fullest extent of the law.

   f. I will pursue you and inform everyone that I meet that you are a rapist, and even if the authorities decide not to prosecute you, I can assure you that I will ruin you at this College, if it's the last thing I do. Ten years from now, when you think you have forgotten me, I will remember you, and just when you think you will never hear from me again, I will be on your doorstep to inform your wife and your children that you are a **rapist!**"

These words may be uncomfortable for you just because you are saying things during a date that you normally would not say. You may be uncomfortable simply because you are not used to being assertive with him. Your new assertiveness may put your relationship with him at risk, simply because he may not be able to handle a woman that he cannot manipulate and control. Face facts. You may lose him, but think of the alternatives. If this guy is thinking of or planning to rape you, anything you can do or say that changes his plans is a victory for you. If he is so intimidated by your assertiveness that he drops you like a hot potato, then do you really want him in your life?

Stage II: Physical maneuvers that work or don't work

There is a difference in the amount of force that generally accompanies date rapes from stranger rapes. Stranger rapists are generally more violent. The stranger rapist is more interested in controlling his victim and gaining power over a woman than in having sex with her. This kind of rapist may resort to violence to exert his power over the woman and physically abuse her along with the actual rape. In many of these cases, there is no penetration or ejaculation.

The date rapist is less likely to use excessive force on his victims as he is often interested in sex. The physical maneuvers that most people associate with repelling a rapist will probably be more effective on the date rapist than on the stranger rapist.

Common physical maneuvers that are thought to be effective:

1. Kicking him in the shins.
2. Slapping his face.
3. Scratching his face.
4. Pulling his hair.

5. Pulling his little finger back to break it.
6. Kicking him in the groin.
7. Pretending to faint.
8. Urinating, defecating, vomiting.
9. Running from him.
10. Screaming "Help! Police! Rape!" or "Fire!"
11. Making a loud noise (I recommend air horns.)
12. Stepping on his foot/instep with high heels.
13. Using a weapon on him (What follows is a partial list of the most common things that people think of as effective weapons against the rapist.)
    a. gun
    b. knife
    c. comb
    d. hair spray
    e. oven cleaner
    f. umbrella
    g. hat pin
    h. car keys
    i. purse/books — whatever is handy
    j. stun guns
    k. tear gas

Many of the physical maneuvers that have been listed above may work on some date rapists since most do not use extreme force to gain control of their victim. These maneuvers, although effective at times in date/acquaintance rape, may not be effective during a stranger rape as there is generally less time to think. Stranger rapists are also more violence-prone and often use lethal weapons. These devices are no match against a gun or knife.

Of course, running, screaming **"FIRE"**, urinating, defecating or vomiting can work whether it is a date or stranger rape.

Some weapons can be very effective in date rape situations because the date rapist is usually not armed and expects little to no resistance to his advances. In all cases **your goal is to incapacitate him long enough for you to escape.** It is important to be realistic in choosing a weapon. Your boyfriend, father or some other man may quickly recommend carrying a gun. Think very carefully if you can use it without hesitation in an assault situation. You may think you can but many women when faced with a criminal cannot effectively use a lethal weapon on him and end up hesitating. This allows the criminal to gain control and confiscate the weapon and use it against her.

Many women in this situation are in such a state of shock when their dates starts to rape them that they do not interpret his actions as rape. This mis-identification of a violent crime may cause additional delay in using a lethal weapon.

In *Real Rape* (How the legal system victimizes women who say no) by Susan Estrich, she talks about why some women do not report being raped by their dates: *"It appears that most women forced to have sex by men they know see themselves as victims, but not as legitimate crime victims."* If a woman doesn't consider herself a "legitimate crime victim," then how could she justify using force to stop the crime? Another reason she may not respond is that it is more difficult for some women to inflict pain on another person. Women for centuries have been taught to help rather than hurt. Jordon and Margaret Paul said it succinctly in their book *Do I Have to Give Up Me to be Loved by You?: "For most of us, the pain we feel is preferable to the pain we fear."*

Most women are not taught as children to be aggressive towards other people. They tend to be more concerned about hurting another's feelings than men are. In fact some women are unfortunately more comfortable receiving pain than giving pain.

In one particularly violent case of rape in Chicago in 1980, a woman was raped in her apartment for more than four hours and although the woman could have hit her assailant with more than a dozen objects within her reach (any one of them could have knocked him unconscious), she could not bring herself to do him bodily harm. This case may sound ludicrous, but in many situations, a woman may find it so difficult to "pull out the stops" and injure her attacker that she either hesitates, or does not do it at all and suffers the consequences. She may also be worried that she can not hurt him enough to stop him so she would rather not risk making him even more angry.

Whatever you decide to do or not do, do not be too hard on yourself. Do not blame yourself or judge yourself too harshly. Rape is a crime of violence and intimidation. Whatever decision you made, you did the best you could under the circumstances. Remember you are the survivor of a violent crime.

According to the *Ms.* study as recorded in the book "I Never Called it Rape" by Robin Warshaw,... *"women who avoided being raped had a lower emotional response to the initial attack—that is, they felt less fear, self blame, helplessness and shock when accosted than did women who were raped. These women also more often ran away and screamed for help."* ("Fire" is potentially a better thing to scream as it invokes a more positive response in bystanders.)

Beyond words...what can you do physically?

1. Quarreling may further provoke the attack.
2. Crying may not work and increases his opinion that you are weak and helpless.
3. Try to remain calm if you can. **Breathe** deeply. This will reduce the shock and get oxygen to your brain which allows you to think more clearly.
4. Think quickly. Is this guy the type who can be reached by talking (try suggestions 15, 16, 17, 18, 19), and reasoning, or will he only respond to physical resistance on your part.
5. Get away from him. If you are in high heels, get them

off. You cannot run in them. If you are not dressed for running (Tight skirt? Get it up above your knees.), make whatever adjustments that are necessary to get away. If it means that you have to run out of his place in your bare feet, don't hesitate. Move and move fast!

6. Run toward light and people or get in a car and lock the doors and hit the horn until someone comes to your rescue.

7. If you are in a parking garage or around a parked car, you can get down and crawl under the parked car. (Scream "fire" from under the car—it will be difficult for him to reach you there.)

8. When you scream "fire" people are much more likely to come to your rescue if they think you are battling a fire.

9. If you are in a gang rape situation and there are people standing around doing nothing or even encouraging the rapist (as happened in New Bedford, Mass.), **look at one person in the eyes, make eye contact with that person and tell him/her to run and get the police.** (It is difficult to motivate a member of a group to leave the group and go for help unless you single him out. No one wants to be the first to do anything. Making direct eye contact with just one person will help that person feel responsible for what is happening to you, especially if he does nothing to stop it.)

10. Telling him you have a venereal disease like AIDS may work in some cases of date rape, however, it may be ineffective in cases of stranger rape.

11. Acting crazy or like you are on drugs and having a hallucination may make you too much for him to deal with.

12. If you can, urinate or defecate on yourself or stick your fingers down your throat and vomit on yourself.

If you are outside, eat grass as it will make you vomit. In short, make yourself as disgusting as possible. This can be effective in cases of date rape as the man is generally more interested in having sex with you than inflicting harm.

13. If all the above fail or is not possible, appear to cooperate. He is not expecting this and may then drop his guard or his weapon. (However, most date rape situations do not involve heavy violence or weapons.)

14. **Thumb to the eyeball push:** When his guard is down, place your hands on each side of his face in a caressing motion. Move your hands toward the corners of his eyes and push your thumbs into the corners of his eyes. He will immediately go into shock, his eyes will pop out of his sockets and you will then have the opportunity to escape. If this is too much for you, then go to #15.

15. **The Testicle Jerk:** If you cannot do #14, then try this: Continue the caressing motion down his body and once he exposes himself, take his testicles in your hands and **squeeze and jerk downward as**

hard as you can. He will scream and may fall to his knees. You now have another opportunity to escape.

16. The use of a non-lethal weapon such as tear gas can incapacitate the attacker long enough for you to escape. Generally, tear gas will interrupt the assault and incapacitate the rapist from a distance of 6 to 8 feet. He will recover in approximately 15 to 30 minutes, but you will be long gone when he does. The effectiveness of any tear gas depends on when it was manufactured and the potency of the chemical. Never purchase tear gas in a retail store. Tear gas should only be obtained from a manufacturer.

Whether you decide to fight or not, giving in to a rapist is nothing to be ashamed of. A rape is a violent crime. It is life threatening. Getting out with your life is your utmost concern.

Remember, you can heal only if you are alive!!!

> *"God grant me the ability to accept the things I cannot change, the courage to change the things I can, and the wisdom to know the difference.*
>
> Reinhold Neibuhr

Chapter Eight: After the Assault, The Second Struggle Begins.

After the rape you are not alone and you do not need to suffer alone.
Your immediate goal after the assault is to get to safety as quickly as possible. Your long term goals are to recover physically-mentally-emotionally, and to take back the control of your body and life so that you can forge a stronger identity as a result of what has happened to you.

Whether you decided to fight with all of your strength, put up some resistance or not fight, you have still been violated. In *Recovering From Rape* by Linda Ledray, she talks about the difficulty many women have in applying unrestrained physical force to stop their attacker. "Women, for the most part, are not taught to resist physical attacks. Women are taught to submit to physical force."

After the assault, be gentle on yourself. Remember, it was not your fault, no matter what you did or did not do. (You may tend to judge yourself for your actions or lack of actions during the assault, but no one, no matter what they have done, deserves to be raped.)

The Most Common Emotional Reactions to Sexual Assault

(The following stages may not occur in the order in which they are listed. See Chapter 10: The Emotional Recovery for a more detailed discussion of these reactions.)

A.	Emotional Shock	The victim feels numb and can't cry.
B.	Disbelief	The victim questions the event. Why me?
C.	Embarrassment	What will people/family think?
D.	Shame	Victim feels dirty.
E.	Guilt	It is my fault. If only I..., etc.
F.	Depression	Victim feels tired and hopeless.
G.	Powerlessness	Victim feels out of control.
H.	Disorientation	Victim feels overwhelmed—can't sit still.
I.	Retriggering	Victim has flashbacks of assault.
J.	Denial	Victim minimizes rape.
K.	Fear	Victim has nightmares, fear of pregnancy, AIDS, V.D., intimacy and may fear she is going crazy.
L.	Anxiety	Victim has trouble breathing, experiences muscle tension, has difficulty sleeping, loss of appetite, nausea, stomach problems, nightmares and may experience bedwetting.
M.	Anger	Victim wants to get even, wants to kill her attacker.

For the Survivor: Immediate and Long Term Priorities for Survival

I. Get to a safe place with supportive people that you can trust if you can.

II. (If you can) Do not shower, bathe, douche, wash your hands, brush your teeth, or use the toilet. (If you do, you will destroy evidence of the assault.)

III. Do not change or destroy clothing.

IV. Do not straighten up your house or apartment (scene of the crime) for as hard as it may be not to clean up, you may destroy important evidence if you do.

V. These are some of the reasons to report the assault:

1. Police can help you get to a safe place and get a medical examination.

2. Reporting the crime can help the police get the guy off the street and keep him from attacking another woman like yourself.

3. It is your right and responsibility. The only reason there are so many rape crisis centers and public support for such victims is because women like you had the courage to come forward and report the assault regardless of the circumstances and/or consequences.

4. Colleges and universities are more likely to take actions to stop date rape if they are convinced that there is a problem. Reporting the rape makes them aware.

5. You may be entitled to compensation. Many states have instituted Victim Compensation Laws in which crime victims can apply for monetary awards from the state to pay for medical exams and physical therapy.

6. Reporting the crime immediately after it occurs will help your credibility; however, even if you do not report, it does not mean the crime did not occur.

7. Reporting the assault will get you in touch with Rape Crisis Centers and counseling centers which you need to do as soon as possible after the crime.

8. Sometimes a rapist will end the assault with a threat that if you report the crime, he will come back and hurt you. Reporting the assault however sends him a message that he cannot intimidate you and puts you back in control.

9. Most threats given by rapists after the assault rarely make good on their threats due to police intervention.

10. Some rapists attack their victims again and again and will not stop their assaults until the police get involved.

11. Reporting the crime does not mean that you necessarily have to prosecute him, but if you report it, you keep your options open in case you decide to prosecute at a later date.

12. Keeping silent can hurt you psychologically and emotionally. It may inhibit your ability to get beyond the trauma because you are trying to hide it. Sooner or later you will have to open up and talk about it which can be very therapeutic.

13. Rape crisis counselors, friends, family, etc. cannot help you unless they know about the incident. There are people out there who have been in your place and can help you get beyond this. **You are not alone!**

You have a choice to make—to do what is best for the rapist or to do what is best for *you!*

Many women do not seek help for various reasons. Among them are their fears that the system will not be sensitive to their needs. They may not be aware of the resources in their area or they may want to minimize the severity of the crime. In date rape situations there may be additional reasons that have to do with the relationship of the victim to the rapist, the status or connections of the rapist to the college or university, or else the guy is so popular on campus that the victim feels no one would believe her. Knowing what to expect when you report the crime can diffuse your fears of the unknown.

If you decide to report the rape, what can you expect? The following is an example of some of the things you can expect when you report the rape to the police. These procedures are taken from *Recovering from Rape* by Linda E. Ledray, R.N., Ph.D. and from *Surviving Sexual Assault* for the Los Angeles Commission on Assaults Against Women. The individual procedures in your area may differ. The crime must be reported in the jurisdiction where the assault occurred. You may not be aware that many communities have psychologically trained investigative units that specialize in rape cases. These people have your interest at heart and will be sensitive to your feelings; these units are more likely to be found in large metropolitan areas where rape is common.

1. CALL TO VERIFY JURISDICTION OF PRECINCT where the crime occurred. In filing a crime report with the police, they will ask you your name, address, place of employment, phone no., date, time, location of the assault, as well as a description of the assailant.

2. They will ask you the details of the assault. This will be difficult but they need to know. What happened? What did he do to you? What did he say to you?

Try to be as accurate as possible and try to recall his exact words. Something he said may seem insignificant, but the police may be able to connect him to other assaults through his words or actions. The accuracy of your statements will also help your case during prosecution.

3. In the case of a stranger rape, you may be asked to look at mugshots and assist in making a composite picture. (Do not be too hard on yourself if you cannot remember what he looks like. You have just come through a life-threatening situation. You may be in shock. Be patient as your memory may come back to you later.)

4. They may ask about your activities before and after the attack. This may seem unnecessary, but again something about your activities before or after might become a clue as to why he singled you out (provided it was a stranger rape).

5. The police are not there to judge you. If any of the questions seem improper or accusatory, you have the right to ask why this information is necessary.

Remember, you did not commit the assault—the rapist did. If the police seem to forget this fact, remind them that you or your actions are not on trial here.

6. If you were drinking or using drugs, it is better to include it into your report now. These detectives are not there to arrest you for your conduct—they are investigating a rape. Besides, if you do not include it now and decide to prosecute later, the rapist's defense attorney may discover it and use this information to discredit your testimony.

7. You may be in such a state of post-trauma shock that it is difficult for you to tell your story. If you would feel more comfortable dealing with a female officer, ask for one. You have that right.

8. Most of this will take place at police headquarters. It will be a lot easier for you if you have a supportive friend such as a female roommate, etc. with you. If you are unable to call, have someone make the call for you.

9. Your first inclination may be to call upon your boyfriend, lover, brother, father or parents to be in the police station with you. If they are totally supportive and can handle it, then they can be enormously helpful to you. However, many victims of rape are shocked at the lack of support and understanding they receive from their loved ones. Their families' embarrassment, fear, anger and guilt may make them behave very inappropriately and uncaringly to you at a time when you are most vulnerable. You do not need to deal with all of their "stuff" right now; you have got enough to deal with. Choose a female friend or Rape Crisis counselor who can understand and **not** judge you or your actions.

10. If it was a stranger rape, you may be asked to identify a suspect in a lineup. This is generally done through a one-way glass or a specially lit room so that the suspect cannot see you.

11. After you make your report, you have the right to police transportation to your home. (If the assault occurred at your home or apartment, you may wish to be taken to a friend's place that will be safer and hold less painful memories.)

12. If you do not hear from the police in one or two days, you have the right to call and ask who the case has been assigned to and what is the current status of the investigation.

13. Keep in touch with the detective/s assigned to your case. If you think of any additional information that was not included in your report, do not hesitate to call them—no matter how insignificant. Everything is important!

69

14. You may also be interviewed by the prosecutors' office, and have to tell your story again and again. The prosecutor will decide whether there is sufficient admissible evidence to issue a formal complaint. Even if the state decides not to prosecute, that does not mean that it did not happen. It may only mean that there is insufficient evidence to gain a conviction.
15. If the state does decide to prosecute, the suspect will be arraigned before a judge. You may or may not be required to attend.
16. If the suspect pleads not guilty, a hearing is set and you may be subpoenaed to testify at this hearing. It should take place within ten days (customarily within 72 hours) after the suspect is arrested, but due to overcrowding in prisons and caseloads for the district attorney's office, delays are common.
17. If the judge presiding at the arraignment decides there is enough evidence, the case may go to trial.
18. The suspect may be arraigned in court or if he pleads guilty the suspect is charged and sentenced.
19. You may not have to attend the pretrial hearing.
20. Your presence is required at the actual trial. The Prosecuting Attorney does not represent you; he/she represents the state because the defendant has broken the laws of the state; however, you are the "STAR" witness for the prosecution. The prosecution is hired by the state not by you.
20. Conviction or acquittal.
21. If he is convicted, the rapist is sentenced.
22. If he is acquitted (due to lack of evidence), it does not mean you were not raped. It only means that the state could not prove it beyond a reasonable doubt.

The trial can be a long and drawn out process. You will need all the support you can get before, during and after the trial. Get in touch with the Rape Crisis Center and the Victim Assistance Program in your area. They can help you know exactly what is happening in court and they may be able to help you with transportation to and from court if you need it. Get counseling or get into a survivors' support group. The local rape crisis center can give you information on the groups in your area.

If you are unhappy with the outcome of the trial, you may wish to sue the rapist for damages. This is a civil suit and requires the services of an attorney which you will have to pay for. This attorney, unlike the District Attorney, represents **you** and not the State.

Even if the assailant has no funds to pay you after a judgement is abtained against him, he is identified and embarrassed as a rapist. He can not own a car or other property in the future—if you "keep the judgement alive."

It is important to understand that the requirements (evidence and degree of proof) are not the same in a civil suit as they are in a criminal proceeding. Even if you lose the criminal case against him, you may win monetary damages from him in a civil court.

The purpose of the preceding chapter is not to overwhelm you with the legal process or scare you into not reporting the crime or prosecuting the rapist, but to let you know what will happen so that you can be prepared and handle it day by day.

Take it one day at a time. You are not alone, you need not suffer alone, and you need not go through the trial alone.

Get all of the professional help you are entitled to.

"Remember, no human condition is ever permanent. Then you will not be overjoyed in good fortune nor too sorrowful in misfortune."
Socrates

Chapter Nine: The Medical Exam

The following chapter is not meant to overwhelm you either, but to inform you of not only what will happen during the medical examination process but also what your rights are. There are four reasons why you need to get a medical exam **Immediately** after the assault:

1. To calculate the extent of your injuries. It is common for the victim of a rape to go into a state of shock and numbness in which she will not realize the extent of her injuries.
2. To settle the fears that you may have about AIDS or V.D.
3. To be tested for unwanted pregnancy.
4. To collect medical evidence for possible future prosecution. This evidence must be gathered as soon as possible. The longer you wait, the more difficult it will be for the doctors to obtain usable specimens.

In *Fighting Back* by Janet Bode, she states how medical evidence can become useless if the exam is not performed within a few hours after the assault...." In 1972, St. Paul-Ramsey Hospital, Minnesota, indicated that testing for semen and sperm after a rape was 95% accurate if performed within 12 hours after the rape." This again confirms the need to get the medical exam as soon as possible after the assault.

I. You have the right to be treated with gentleness and sensitivity during the evidentiary exam.

Where do you go to get the examination?
If you decide to report the rape to the police, they will know which hospitals have the services that you need. They can also put you in touch with the Rape Crisis Center for counseling. If you decide not to report it, then you can call your family doctor for advice as to where to go. Any hospital that deals with sexual assaults will hopefully have a sensitively trained team of doctors, nurses and psychologists which can make all the difference in the world during your recovery.

II. You have the right to call your personal physician to be with you during this procedure.

It is a good idea for you to call a supportive friend to come with you or meet you at the hospital. Have your friend bring an extra set of clothes for you as your present clothes may be taken from you and used as evidence of the assault. You may want to have a female friend meet you as she may be more supportive than a boy friend or family member right now.

Waiting in the hospital: Unfortunately, you may not be a high priority in an emergency room, especially if there are no outward signs of physical abuse. This may mean that you will have to wait until the emergency staff gets around to you. The emergency room may not be warm, comfortable or at all pleasant for you especially at this time. In fact it will probably be bright, cold and impersonal. Although the staff should be understanding and supportive, do not count on it. It is possible that they may be cold, impersonal, factual and totally insensitive to your needs and feelings. You may get this not only from males but also from females whom you would think would rally around you to give you support. This is why having a trusting, supportive friend to accompany you during this exam is important. This person can also speak up for your rights when you are incapable of doing so.

III. You have the right to privacy during the collection of medical evidence. If you are a minor, you have the right to request the exam without parents or guardians present.

IV. You have the right to request that police officers leave the examination room during the actual exam.

V. You have the right to have a friend, a family member or a Rape Crisis Counselor present (in the room with you) during the exam.

VI. You have the right to have each procedure explained in detail before you allow the doctors to continue with the exam.

Make sure you understand what the doctors and nurses are telling you. If you cannot decipher the medical terminology, ask them to stop and explain it to you. The doctors and/or medical personnel may ask the following questions or require these additional exams prior to the evidentiary exam:

1. Your medical history.
2. A urine sample for pregnancy testing.
3. What is your recent sexual history?
4. What is your marital status?
5. Are you a virgin?
6. Are you currently using birth control?
7. What was the date of your last period?

8. Is your menstrual cycle regular?
9. Have you ever been pregnant? If so, did you have a live birth, miscarriage or abortion?
10. What was the date of your last sexual intercourse prior to the assault?
11. Do you have children? If so, what are their ages?
12. Was the attacker using a condom?

You may find some of these questions personal and private, but understand that their procedures and testing depend upon your answers.

The Evidentiary Exam

The evidentiary exam is an examination for the purpose of obtaining evidence of sexual assault. It may include a pelvic exam. If forced sodomy or forced oral sex was performed, additional exams may be required of other parts of your body.

The evidentiary exam will document the following: (A) evidence of recent sexual intercourse, if any, (B) evidence of signs of force, (C) evidence that will identify and incriminate the assailant.

(A) Evidence of Recent Sexual Intercourse: The proof of recent sexual intercourse will be obtained by a collection of the following:

   a. seminal fluids
   b. sperm
   c. vaginal secretions
   d. secretions from bodily areas involved in the rape, i.e. vagina, rectum, mouth
   e. samples of pubic hair

The absence of sperm does not mean that intercourse did not occur as many rapists are sexually dysfunctional, at least during the rape, and do not ejaculate during the assault.

(B) Evidence of Force: It is important that evidence be obtained to establish proof that you did not consent to sexual intercourse with the rapist. The following steps may be taken:

   a. Photographs of bruises, abrasions and injuries Since bruises often do not appear for 24–48 hours, you may wish to request that the police take a second set of pictures at a later date when they become visible. (These pictures are useless as evidence if you take them yourself.)

   b. Torn or soiled clothing worn during the rape will be held by the police for evidence. If you want it back, you will need to ask for it.
   Lack of physical signs of force does not mean that force was not used. Date rapists often use minimal physical force but *will* use extreme emotional and mental intimidation to get you to submit to their desires and maintain control—long after the rape.

   c. Blood samples may be taken to ascertain whether drugs and/or alcohol are in your system. This is likely if you indicate that you've used drugs, or they find evidence of drug use. This evidence can show that you were not in control of your faculties at the time of the rape. Some women are actually drugged without their knowledge at parties and are later raped. **Pour your own drinks!**

(C) Evidence that will identify and incriminate the assailant

This physical evidence is needed to build a case against the rapist. It may start to disintegrate with the passage of time. Some of the physical evidence may also disintegrate because of the weather. If you were raped outside, there may be physical signs of the attack that will disintegrate because of the weather. If you were raped outside, there may be physical signs of the attack that will be destroyed if it rains. This is another good reason to report the assault to the police as soon as possible.

The following steps may be taken to help build the state's case against the assailant. You should remember that once criminal charges have been filed, it becomes a case of the State versus the rapist. Perhaps one day the victim will also be able to have representation by an additional attorney to the state's attorney, but that time has not arrived.

A collection of the following will help during prosecution:
1. Seminal fluids to determine the rapist's blood type.
2. Foreign matter still on your body such a leaves, fibers, hairs, etc. that will be used to identify your attacker.

VII. You have the right to request copies of all medical reports.

VIII. You have the right to contact the Victim Witness Program and be reimbursed for these expenses (if available in your area) and you have the right to request help in filling out the necessary forms to qualify for financial assistance.

IX. You have the right to strict medical confidentiality.

Pregnancy Testing

A urine specimen will be taken to determine if you were pregnant before the rape. You should be tested again to determine if you have become pregnant as a result of the rape. Some states will pay for this follow-up exam if you have reported the rape within 36 hours of the assault as part of the Evidentiary Exam.

*The National Center for the Prevention and Control of Rape have indicated that <u>women rarely become pregnant as the result of rape</u>. If you do become pregnant, you may decide to have an abortion, place the child up for adoption or keep the child.

X. You have the right to make the decision as to whether to keep the child or abort without being pressured by family, friends, clergy or therapists. This is your decision and yours alone.

This decision is an important one. Seek advice from the Rape Crisis Center and other qualified professionals who will continue to support you long after the decision, whatever it may be. One fact that some women may overlook in their desire to keep the child because of religious convictions is that this child even before birth may become a negative reminder of the rape and the rapist. Your attitude about the incident and the attacker can influence your attitude about the pregnancy. This anger and hatred toward your attacker can be very therapeutic; however, if it is transferred to your child it can be harmful.

XI. You have the right to the common reactions of rape victims such a sleeplessness, nightmares, anxiety and fear and *not* have these reactions considered abnormal behavior by those who do not understand what you are going through.

XII. Above all, you have the right to survive.

Remember, rape is an act of violence. It is a life-threatening situation. Anything that you did to save your life, whether it was to fight back or submit due to extreme force or fear of force, you did the best you could! Your Rape Crisis counselor can do much to help you get into support groups so that you can understand that **you are not alone.** This has happened to many women and they have faced the same questions, doubts and fears that will undoubtedly plague you as you start your recovery.

XIII. You have the right to not be judged by other people who have not gone through what you have. It did not happen to them and they have no right to judge you!

If you are alive, you are not a victim...you are a survivor! You may not be able to believe this right now, but keep telling yourself...
"I am a survivor!"
"I am a survivor!"
"I will make it through this!
"I will survive!"

"Time and love can heal all of my wounds."

> *"Never are we nearer the Light than when the darkness is deepest."*
>
> Vivekananda

Chapter Ten: The Emotional Recovery

Long after the physical body has healed from the assault, the emotional and mental healing will continue. Some experts and psychologists have indicated that the emotional impact of date rape can continue for years after the rape.

Don't give up five minutes before the miracle!

The emotional recovery from date rape often takes a lot longer than if it was a stranger rape situation. This is because there is an unspoken bond of trust which exists in every dating situation; this is destroyed when he rapes her. This destruction of trust is very serious and substantially inhibits the normal healing process. When that trust has been violated, it takes a lot longer for a woman to trust men whether she knows them or not. Most women are familiar with the possibility of assault from the stranger but not from men they know and trust. That is what makes date/acquaintance rape so insidious!

It's not your fault!
no matter how stupid you may feel,
no matter if you knew the guy,
no matter if you were high on drugs/alcohol,
no matter if you originally said yes, then said **no,**
no matter if you've had sex with him before,
no matter if no one believes you,
no matter if you choose not to report it,
no matter what happened, **It's not your fault!!!**

It is important to remember that *he* made a deliberate choice to take from you your most precious possession, your privacy, your sense of safety, your trust, and your control of your life and body. It was not your fault. He was perfectly able to stop. He simply chose not to, no matter what you said or did.

The emotional roller coaster that happens after a date rape can last for years; however, the length of recovery can be reduced if you get professional help for yourself. It is natural to want to deny what has happened and get on with the rest of your life. However, the fears, anger, rage, panic attacks, feelings of worthlessness and the occasional feeling that you may be going crazy cannot be buried or denied for long. Sooner or later these feelings will surface and when they do, they may adversely affect your other relationships, especially with lovers, husbands, friends or family. Your job and your ability to function at school may also be affected. Going back to school can be very traumatic since many victims of date rape will come into contact with their attackers again when they return.

Getting help from a qualified rape crisis counselor or therapist will help you deal with the complex and potentially self-destructive feelings that you may be going through and can also be of help when you run into him again.

The Most Common Reactions to Sexual Assault
There is no normal/abnormal, good/bad, right or wrong response to rape. Much of a woman's reactions may depend upon her level of self worth before the assault as well as the resources available to her at the time of the attack. Her family dynamics (whether she will be blamed or shunned for being raped) and the amount of sincere support and caring that friends show after the rape will also greatly affect the healing process.

• The following reactions are not necessarily in order. Each woman experiences these at different intervals. You may stay in one stage for a long time or may even skip one of the stages entirely. If you feel like you are stuck in a particular stage for a long time, your counselor/ therapist or support group may be able to help you understand why you are stuck or even help you get through it. In *Recovering From Rape* by Linda E. Ledray, R.N., Ph.D., she indicates some of the stages you may face.

(1) **Emotional Shock and Disbelief**—the "Why Me?" Stage: You may believe that rape cannot happen to good girls or that a rapist cannot possibly be a guy you know.

If you believe the male created myths that women who are raped, want it, provoke it or deserve it, you may be in shock and it may be more difficult for you to believe that the rape actually happened to you. You may not be able to cry. You may feel numb. You may block out the rape and find it difficult to remember anything but the time before or after the rape. As you begin to get stronger and more emotionally able to deal with the assault, flashbacks and/or nightmares may start to occur. You may also feel weak, have trouble sleeping and be exhausted.

(2) **Embarrassment, shame and guilt:** "I'm ashamed of telling anyone." "I don't think they'll believe me." "I can't tell my parents; they'd think I made it up." These are some of the things that women say when they are feeling shame, guilt or embarrassment about a date rape situation. Feeling embarrassed about being raped is just another way of beating up on yourself. It is a way of taking responsibility for the man's behavior. Women throughout the centuries have not only suffered the rape and abuse of men, but they have also been ostracized for being victims by their husbands and families.

In *Against Our Will* by Susan Brownmiller, she tells the tragic story of the women and children of Bangladesh. In March of 1971, 200,000 to 400,000 women and girls were raped by Pakistani troups who were in Bangladesh to put down a rebellion. The majority of the women were Moslems and so many of the husbands refused to take them back into the family because they were considered "defiled and unclean" after they had been touched by other men. Their families added to their horror by banish-

ing them because of the "shame on the family honor." It did not make any difference that the women had been kidnapped, assaulted, raped and abused at gunpoint by enemy soldiers.
   Your husband, boyfriend, family or friends may not understand. Find a friend who does.
   There is nothing for you to be ashamed of. You are *not* the rapist - he is. He is the one who should be ashamed!

(3) **Disorientation:** You may feel disoriented and confused by all that has happened to you as well as being inundated by the demands being put upon you at this time. There are decisions that have to be made, important decisions, and even though you are in no emotional condition to think rationally, you still have to make them. This is another reason to contact a Rape Crisis counselor and/or support group who can empathize with what you are going through. **Remember, you are not alone.**

(4) **Anger, Rage and Thoughts of Revenge:** It is perfectly acceptable and normal to be angry with your attacker. In fact it can be very healthy to be angry, because anger can become a motivating force out of the feelings of helplessness, powerlessness and worthlessness. Often the feelings of anger and rage do not come until later which is unfortunate, because it can be easier to make decisions about your welfare if you have the energy of anger. You may also have thoughts and fantasies of elaborate revenge. Do not be too concerned about these feelings and fantasies - they are natural, considering what you have been through.

(5) **Depression:** During the next few days after the assault, you may experience a severe depression. The severity of the feelings after the rape may be confusing to you especially if you are being told by other people that "You're okay, just forget about it." "You're not hurt so what's the big deal?" The tendencies of families and other

men (even though they may love you and have the best of intentions in mind) is to minimize what has happened to you. This is a defense mechanism that enables them to get on with their lives and deal with the fact that they may be feeling guilty for your assault. If they can convince you that the rape is no big thing, then they can forget about it.

Some of your girlfriends may also minimize the assault or even blame you because they feel that if you are an innocent victim, then maybe it can happen to them. So it is easier to blame you and not the rapist whom they know and in this way they feel safer. Recently a family from a small town in Georgia was attacked and murdered in their beds. The whole town could not accept the randomness of the attack so they made up the story that there were drugs in the house. This lie made them feel like they could prevent being murdered by just not using drugs. They felt safer if the victims were somehow guilty. In this way too, your friends may feel safer on campus if they believe you caused the attack or made it up. Your friends and family may even tell you that they are sick of talking about the incident. This is also a way of denying that what happened was important and worth remembering.

The primary fear during a rape is not forced sex, but a fear of being killed!!! A common reaction to being in a life-threatening situation is to become depressed. Depression may cause you to feel the following: (1) You may be discouraged about the future. (2) You may feel that you have nothing to live for or that things are hopeless. (3) You may also exaggerate your faults and see only the worst side of yourself.

Depression can be self perpetuating in that the more you look for the worst side of yourself, the more you are depressed. This feeling of sadness can last for an extended period of time especially after a date rape. When women are raped, they have a fear of the rapist and anyone that resembles the rapist. In a date rape situation, a woman's trust of men she knows is destroyed. This can lead to a total lack of trust in any and all men, no matter what they look like. She may lump all men together as potential rapists. Even boyfriends, lovers and husbands are not immune to being considered in the same category as the rapist. It may be difficult for her to trust men. She may distrust her ability to differentiate a good (safe) man from a bad (dangerous) man.

(6) Retriggering: This is when something or someone reminds you of the rape. Often on the one year anniversary of the assault, the survivor will have an emotional reaction. Some women break down in tears on the anniversary even though on a conscious level they were not aware that it had been one year. This can also happen if the rape occurred in a particular place like a parking garage in which case all parking garages would become dangerous. This would likely cause an emotional reaction, because it reminds the woman of where she was raped. Again in date rape this can become an even more difficult reoccurrence because the rapist is often in contact with the victim after the rape. So the trauma is even greater because the victim may have continual retriggering incidents. This is why in some cases the emotional terror of continual contact with the rapist may cause the victim to leave school just to get away and stop the memories from reoccurring.

(7) Other Reactions to Date Rape: You may become more dependent on friends and family or you may feel compelled to withdraw from people for safety reasons. It is common to have low self-esteem and to change your appearance so as to repel anyone that might be interested in you sexually.

We all have these thoughts from time to time but in most cases these are temporary feelings of despair and quickly pass. However, when a life-threatening crisis like rape occurs, everything is serious and nothing should be taken for granted.

If thoughts of suicide or self harm occur, realize that they are normal but a Rape Crisis counselor or therapist should be consulted at once.

Sexual dysfunction and/or promiscuity can also occur. It is obvious why sexual dysfunction occurs, i.e. sex becomes synonymous with rape. If promiscuity occurs after a rape, it can be the most difficult for friends and family to understand and often gives them an excuse to disbelieve her story (which is more comfortable for them anyway).

Perhaps one of the most famous cases of acquaintance rape appears to have happened to Jessica Hahn, the church secretary who was allegedly maneuvered into a private hotel room and subsequently raped by Jim Bakker, evangelist to the PTL Club. What appears to have happened fits the acquaintance rape scenario. To Jessica Hahn, Jim Bakker could not have been held in higher respect or authority than to be the pastor of her church. (Talk about ultimate trust!) After Bakker admitted to having an affair with Ms. Hahn, he then tried to convince everyone that she was a prostitute hired to seduce him. This kind of response, that of trying to defend the actions of rape by discrediting the victim is typical of men who are accused of raping someone they know.

Many women still believe that "good girls" do not get raped and so if a woman is raped by her date or by a friend, she probably asked for it, turned the guy on and then changed her mind or made the whole thing up to begin with.

Many people have rigid expectations of the way a woman is supposed to behave after she has been raped. If her behavior is not consistent with what a rape victim is supposed or expected to be, then there is something wrong with her story. If she doesn't act hysterical, if she isn't sobbing, if her clothes aren't shredded, if she isn't black and blue from fighting off her rapist, then she's got to be lying or she must have asked for it.

Many people, family, friends, pastors, husbands and

others will often get fed up with a woman's inability to "forgive and forget" and get on with her life. Forgiveness, which is the ultimate healer, cannot be embraced until she has worked through all of her other feelings in connection with the assault. This includes anger, rage, hatred, fear, depression and helplessness. There are no easy answers to recovery from this devastating crime. Many times religeous people will offer flip Bible verses, although they probably mean well, this will only alienate her and drive her feelings inside.

Ms. Hahn had the sympathies of many men and women when she revealed her story, but I am sure some of her supporters changed their minds when she posed for *Playboy* magazine. I heard several people say that since she didn't behave the way an "innocent rape victim" would have behaved, that they doubted if indeed she had really been raped! Perhaps Jessica Hahn did not react the way they expected her to act. However, women react in different ways after they have been raped, depending on many factors, such as:

(1) Her level of self worth before the attack.
(2) The extent of her relationship with her attacker.
(3) The violence of the assault.
(4) Her feelings about the assault and the level of self-blame she engages in.
(5) Whether she reports the assault and decides to prosecute the rapist.
(6) The way she is treated by law enforcement and medical personnel.
(7) Whether she gets professional help after the attack.
(8) The amount of caring and support she receives from those whom she values and trusts in her life (family and friends). All these things will impact her recovery and impact her behavior after the rape. Some women engage in frequent sex or may even get involved in pornography which may subconsciously lower the value of what has been taken from them. Other women have such feelings of worthlessness

that they no longer value themselves or their body. This attitude of low self-worth may cause an escalation in promiscuity or a recreation of victimization.

If she feels like the only thing of value in her life has already been taken from her against her will, then why not? A common practice among pimps is to rape young girls repeatedly as a prelude to coercing the girls to work for them. Whatever Ms. Hahn's reasons were for posing for *Playboy,* her actions after the rape have nothing to do with the rape. It does not change what has happened to her. We must not judge her. No one who has survived a rape, whether by her lover, date, acquaintance, stranger or even by her minister deserves to be judged as guilty. What she needs, as do all rape survivors, is support, understanding and prayers for her recovery.

"Men never do evil so completely and cheerfully as when they do it from religious conviction."
—Blaise Pascal (1623–62)

Rape is the only crime in which society tends to blame the victim.

Before we judge her, let us see our daughter, our sister, our mother, ourselves. Let us give only help, understanding and caring for she, in her pain, is us.

Priorities:

First of all, determine your priorities

1) Get to physical safety!
2) Get some help! (Rape Crisis counselors, therapists, etc.)
3) After you have reported the assault to the proper authorities, get a medical exam.
4) Give yourself some time off. You need time to recuperate. You may tend to want to forget the rape and get back to work or school as if nothing

happened. This is denial and will eventually only inhibit or prolong your emotional healing. Sooner or later the trauma will surface consciously or unconsciously and keep surfacing until you take the time and energy to deal with it. Remember you have been through a life-threatening situation. Just like with a physical injury to the body you need time to heal. The mind and heart need time to heal as well. Just because you cannot see the emotional injuries doesn't mean they have not occurred.

5) Start your healing process by realizing that you have choices. Choices as to how you react and how you view the assault.

6) Keep repeating that it was not your fault. The tidal wave of feelings that are happening to you now do not have to incapacitate you, if you realize that in order to get a handle on your feelings you must first change the way you think.

• It may be impossible for you to think about this right now but when you are ready, when you start to become more independent and able to think about putting your life back together again, try working on the following life changing ideas.

Dr. Wayne Dyer, in his book *Your Erroneous Zones* (which I really recommend) talks about choosing how you will feel. "Feelings are not just emotions that happen to you. Feelings are reactions you **choose** to have. If you are in charge of your own emotions, you don't have to choose self-defeating reactions."

You have the power to control what thoughts you give power to. Thoughts about the rape and the rapist will continue to pop into your head from time to time, but recognize that it is up to you to decide as to what extent they immobilize you. Some women, who have never gotten over the rape and have never had professional

counseling, cannot seem to ever get the rape out of their minds. The rape and rapist continue to plague their thoughts for years. For these women, the rapist still has power over them. He is still raping them, not their bodies, but their peace of mind, their safety, their security, their trust and their sense of dignity and self worth.
Listen to yourself.
The prophet Elijah was instructed to go to a mountain top to speak with God. When he arrived, he discovered that the Divine presence was not in the earthquake, nor in the wind, nor in the fire, but in "a still small voice." It is the same for you now. That Devine presence is also within you. You can access that inner voice once you become quiet and listen. That same inner voice that can also keep you out of dangerous situations, can give you the guidance that you will need to make it through each day. Listen to that voice. **You are not alone.**

"Let us be silent, that we may hear the whispers of the gods."
— Emerson

If you don't control your thoughts, who does?

If you do not take control of your own thoughts, then *he* (the rapist) is still in control of you. First, you have a thought then the thought is followed by a feeling. **Rape is a crime of power over another person. During the rape the rapist takes your power away from you by force or intimidation. After the rape, take back your own power. Do not give it to him.** If you want to change your feelings, change your thoughts.

Common thought has it that other people make us happy or sad, but this is not accurate. You make yourself happy or unhappy based on the thoughts that you think. I am not minimizing what has happened to you. You have every right to the feelings that are going on inside of you, but recovery lies in changing your thoughts from those of a victim to those of a survivor...and finally to those of a **winner!**

This process is not a quick one; it is going to take some time. Our self image and self worth are built slowly from childhood to the present time. Children come into this life with a wonderful self image. It changes only with constant conditioning that they are not worthy or good enough the way they are. To change the mind requires constant reconditioning that you are beautiful and worthy of the best that life has to offer.

Now that you have realized that you can control your thoughts, it is time to start reprogramming your mind with positive information.

"All that we are is a result of what we have thought."
— Abraham Lincoln

What is an affirmation? An affirmation is a positive thought that you consciously focus on in order to produce a desired result. The affirmation is a simple yet powerful technique that can heal and transform your most deeply held beliefs.

How do affirmations work? (1) Your life is a reflection of your prominent thoughts and beliefs. (2) Change your thoughts and beliefs about yourself and others and you change your world. (3) The words you speak and write are directly related to the thoughts you think.

How to create healing affirmations:

1) Decide what needs to be healed in your life.

2) What would it feel like if this area of your life were healed?

3) Using "I", create a positive statement that gives you the desired result.

    a. Write your affirmation in the present tense as if the experience were happening now, like, "I am becoming more peaceful each day!" If you're having trouble even concentrating on "peace" try getting your rage out by decorating a pillow to symbolize

92

the rapist and beat it until your rage is expended or until you're exhausted.

    b. Write your affirmation positively. If you say "I am not angry!" the subconscious mind filters out the "not" and hears only "I am angry!" Restate it by saying "I am releasing my rage and anger each day in an appropriate way!"

4) Write your affirmation, then say it several times. Finally get quiet and feel it. How do you feel when you say it? Do you feel good about it? If you do not, alter the words until it feels right.

5) Repeat your affirmations daily - morning and evening.

6) Add one statement to your affirmation: "This or something better is now created for me for the highest good of all concerned!"

7) Your affirmation will release negative beliefs. These beliefs are from your subconscious mind. They are the blocks that will keep your affirmations from happening. When they come up, write them down, and burn them daily or weekly - whichever is appropriate. Remember your mind does not change its belief system overnight - **It takes time!** Be patient with yourself, for if you really want to change your life, it will happen, but it will take some time.

"Behold, I show you a mystery. We shall not all sleep, but we shall all be changed."
— I Corinthians 15:51

    The following statements can change your thoughts if you repeatedly say them to yourself and post them on your mirror and around your environment. Challenge any thought or comment that opposes them. The following affirmations will help you regain your power. Use one or all or make some up that feel good to you, but above all, use them every day and be consistent. The affirmation is a simple yet powerful technique that can heal and transform your deeply held beliefs.

I am beautiful!

I am worthy of love!

I am important!

I am even now surviving this!

I am getting stronger every day!

I am always safe from harm!

I am responsible for my own thoughts!

I can control my own thoughts!

I can change my thoughts!

I have charge of my feelings, because I control my thoughts!

My feelings are healthy and cause me to take action to make this a useful day.

I have control as to how long this incident will affect me!

I will use this incident to help other women prevent being raped!

I can learn to think differently about anything!

I am determined to be victorious over this incident!

I am determined to be happy!

I will challenge and destroy all thoughts that create immobilizing behavior!

I have power over my life each and every day!

I am determined to get all the help I need, because I believe in myself!

I am guiltless!

I deserve to be treated with gentleness and respect!

I am learning to love myself more and more each day!

These are a few of the positive statements that you can program into your mind that will change the direction of your life and especially give you more control of your feelings. Your brain is composed of ten billion billion working parts. It has enough capacity to accept ten new facts every second.

The human brain can store an amount of information equivalent to one hundred trillion words and that is only using a tiny fraction of the storage space. **Your words do have power!** The mind is like a computer—to change the output, you have to change the incoming data. The incoming data is the hundreds of thousands of messages that you keep telling you about yourself each day.

Some of the negative messages that you may have said about yourself are: "I am no good," "I'm stupid," "I probably deserved to be raped anyway," "Why didn't I fight back?" "I should've known that he was going to rape me. Why didn't I run?", etc.

These kinds of self-defeating, immobilizing thoughts and words will only tend to keep you a prisoner of the assault - and the man who committed it.

If you want to change your feelings, change your thoughts.

If you want to change your life, change your thoughts about you.

Self worth cannot be verified by others.

You are worthy because you say it is so. If you depend on others for your value it is not self-worth, it is other-worth.

I strongly recommend hypnosis to gain control over your own thoughts and emotions. A sleep therapy audiotape can help to quiet fears and reestablish your sense of security.

Change is not instantaneous, at least not positive change. It will take time to change the way you think about yourself. While you are working on you, get some professional help such as a Rape Crisis counselor or therapist so that you can deal with the occasional trauma when the flashbacks occur.

In this chapter I have talked about the mental and emotional healing, but there is another aspect of ourselves that I have not talked about. This is the spiritual recovery.

Many years ago, women who were raped were not only shunned by their families, friends and husbands, but in some cultures the prevalent belief was that she had "sinned against God" and was therefore being punished. No belief is as destructive to a woman's self worth as this.

If you are a religious person, you may be torturing yourself with these kinds of feelings. **There is no justification, either religious or otherwise, in believing that your rape is God's punishment.** This would make the rapist God's Messenger. Rape is not an act of God. It is an act of violence and intimidation against not only a woman's body, but also against her very soul. Whether you are of the Christian, Jewish or Moslem faith, God is good, God is Love and no loving God would condone or excuse the act of rape.

This time of recovery can be a time to reflect inward. Pray, meditate, ask for peace of mind and the help you need to heal your intense pain. There is no rationalization why God allows these things to happen, but even though we are at a loss as to why it happened, you can have the assurance that God will be there with you through the tears and the feelings of loneliness and despair.

You are truly not alone. Use this mediation every day — morning and evening.

The light of God surrounds me; the love of God enfolds me; the power of God protects me; the presence of God watches over me; wherever I am, God is.

One night a woman had a dream. She dreamed she was walking along the beach with the Lord. Across the sky flashed scenes from her life. For each scene, she noticed two sets of footprints in the sand; one belonged to her, and the other to the Lord.

When the last scene of her life flashed before her, she looked back at the footprints in the sand. She noticed that many times along the path of her life there was only one set of footprints. She also noticed that it happened at the very lowest and saddest times of her life. This really bothered her and she questioned the Lord about it. "Lord, you said that once I decided to follow you, you'd walk with me all the way. But I have noticed that during the most troublesome times of my life, there is only one set of footprints. I don't understand why when I needed you most, you would leave me."

The Lord replied, "My precious, precious child, I love you and would never leave you. During your times of trial and suffering, when you see only one set of footprints, it was then that I carried you."

—(*Footprints,* author unknown)

(I recommend *The Greatest Miracle in the World* by Og Mandio, especially "The Memo From God," and *Words That Heal* by Douglas Bloch.

> *"Let me walk three weeks in the footsteps of my enemy, carry the same burden, have the same trials as he, before I say one word to criticize."*
>
> An Indian Chief's Prayer

Chapter Eleven: Man to Man

Although this book is primarily for women, I could not write a book about date rape without saying something to men in general. I am not a woman and I have never been raped. Although I have never raped anyone, I also know that it is almost impossible to grow up as a male in this society and not think about or fantasize about the act of rape. Does that make me a rapist? **No!** Thinking about rape does not make you a rapist. We all have thoughts and fantasies of a sexual nature that if made public would cause us a lot of embarrassment and shame. In talking to many men about this book, I ran into a common series of responses.

From a man's perspective, at least those that I have talked to, they are concerned about the following:

(A) They are concerned about "the women who lead them on, tease them, and then when the man has reached his sexual peak, the women say no."

(B) They also seem to be concerned that women may be claiming "rape" to get even with a guy she wants to hurt, thereby ruining his reputation.

Before I discounted these concerns, I listened to them and analyzed what I thought was their logic.

In (A), men seem to be saying what has been said for thousands of years, that "A man is not really responsible for his actions beyond a certain point and that if a woman wants to avoid being raped, she shouldn't turn the man on to such a degree so that he can't stop himself." In questioning the men about their ability to control their sexual arousal, I asked them if there had been any occasion in their lives in which they had to abruptly stop during sexual intercourse, regardless of the degree of arousal. In one case, the man had been heavily petting his girlfriend in high school when his mother came home unexpectedly and surprized them in the act. What was interesting about this scenario is that the girlfriend had tried to get him to stop without success. He said "I'm too turned on to stop now," but when his mother walked in on them, he somehow found the control to stop immediately. In fact, he said that his erection was gone almost at once.

There is no point at which a man cannot control himself during sexual arousal. He may not *want* to control himself, but he can stop if he has to or if he wants to!

Let's make this a bit more personal and take it a step further. Suppose you (a man) were out of work, had no money, hadn't worked for a long time and money was all you could think about. You dreamed about it every night. Your creditors were banging on your door and harrassing you daily.

You had to have some money. So you went to the bank and asked for a loan, which they refused. You then went up to the teller's window and watched her count the money on the other side of the counter. When you felt like you could not take it anymore, you grabbed a handful of bills from the teller and ran out of the bank.

Did you commit a crime? Would the bank prosecute you? Would you expect to go to jail if caught? I hope you would answer yes, because you did indeed break the law and the consequences for your actions are that you will go to a state penitentiary for a number of years. Do you see the analogy?

If we use the example of robbing a bank, then perhaps you can see that even though you needed the money and were in debt, you committed a crime. Even though you felt the bank "tempted you" with all that money laying around, you still took what did not belong to you and committed a felony.

Likewise, when you are on a date with a woman and get physically turned on, that does not give you the right to take what does not belong to you. You may feel that she should not be a tease and turn you on or that she should not drink and get you so worked up that you cannot stop. If you don't like the way you are being manipulated—then get up and leave. You are always in control. You always have a choice. It does not matter what you think at this point. We all have thoughts and fantasies of robbing a bank and getting away with it. No one will put you in jail for robbing a bank in your mind, but the minute you decide to act out your fantasy, you have committed a crime and can go to jail.

Beyond getting caught and what happens to you, think about the woman. You physically hurt no one but you if you commit rape in your mind. However the minute you physically commit a rape, you have abused and scarred a woman for the rest of her life.

If you are obsessed with thoughts of rape, you may need to seek professional help (psychologist, psychiatrist, school counselor) to stop the momentum from thoughts changing into actions. Criminals start their life of crime in their thoughts before their actions get them into trouble with the law. **Remember, you are what you think!**

Take responsibility for your actions. No one turns you on—you turn yourself on with the thoughts that are going on in your head. The thoughts are yours, not hers. You have control over them, not her. You can change your thoughts, you can continue to think about her, about how you want to "make it with her," and get yourself all worked up so that your conscience cannot reach you anymore, but realize that **you turn yourself on** and you must take full responsibility for your thoughts and actions.

Just like the man in the bank, he did not break the law

until he took the money. You do not break the law until you persist in your sexual advances after she says no or after she is incapacitated so that her ability to say no is impaired. In other words, if you go into the bank and get their permission to take money out of the bank (bank loan), then you have not broken the law. If you go into the bank and take the money without their consent, you are a thief. If you go into a bank and set off a bomb that puts everyone to sleep or incapacitates them so they they cannot stop you from stealing the money, then you are also a thief and will go to jail.

After she says no, it's rape!

If you have sex with a person and they cannot give their consent due to being incapacitated by alcohol, drugs or otherwise unconscious, **you have committed rape.**

A woman has the right to say no at any time without fearing the consequences.

If you have sex with a person and get their unwilling consent or lack of resistance due to your verbal, physical or emotional threats, then you have made it impossible for her to say no and **you have committed rape.** Just as a man has the right to "pull out" in the middle of intercourse regardless of what a woman wants, so a woman has the same right to stop the sexual activities at any time, regardless of your wants.

If you feel that a woman is teasing you and playing with your emotions, then rather than risk a rape situation with her (which could land you in jail and ruin her life and yours), sit down and talk to her and say:

1) "Look, I don't appreciate the way I'm being treated."

2) "I'm getting a lot of mixed messages from you. It seems one minute you want to have sex and the next minute, you don't. What's going on?"

3) "I want you to know that this is your decision too and I'm not going to take advantage of you, but please be honest with me and tell me what you want. Yes? or No?"

In (B), the men were concerned that a woman would ruin their reputation. They also believed that in a dating situation many women really wanted it, but after the sex, they would make up the fact that they were raped to get even with the man.

It would be difficult for a man to understand the trauma of reporting a rape, unless he has either been raped himself by another man or his girlfriend, sister or wife was raped and he was forced to witness the ordeal.

No one in their right mind would make up a rape and go through all of the terror and trauma of reporting it to the police, taking the medical exam and exposing herself to the aftermath of insinuations and abuse by friends and family, unless it had actually occurred.

It is hard for men to grasp what a woman goes through at the time of the rape and of the ongoing trauma that can last for years unless he has himself been raped.

For a man to think about himself being raped by a woman can be a pleasant fantasy; however, women hardly ever rape men. What is more likely to happen to a man is to be raped by another man. (A man is more likely to be raped by another man than by a woman.)

Imagine yourself going out with a bunch of guys. Maybe you all go to a football game, have a great time and afterwards you all go to a local bar for a few drinks. On the way home, the guys take you out to a vacant lot and hold you down and brutally rape you for four or five hours. Then for good measure, they beat you up, kick you and tell you that if you ever tell anyone, they will finish you off. You lie there in the vacant lot, cut, bleeding, every inch of your body hurts. You stagger to your feet but are not able to stand. Suddenly you get violently ill and vomit. You are finally able to get to a gas station and try to tell someone. You tell the guys that work there that you have been raped by four men and they laugh and run you out of the station calling you a fag. You finally tell your story to the police and they question whether you are a homosexual and snicker about your manhood. They say "There's no way any guy's gonna do that to me. I'd kill him first!", "Why didn't you fight back?", "What're ya doin' goin' out with a bunch of queers for anyway?" You try to explain that you did not know what they were, but you stop. You figure what's the use; they'll never believe you anyway....

There is no evidence that indicates that male homosexuals go around committing rape against heterosexuals. The majority of rapes are committed by male heterosexuals.*

*(The preceding statement is not meant to cast aspersions on gay people but to give you an idea of how insensitive some people can be toward rape victims, whether male or female.)

You tell them that you did not really even know them. You try and try to get someone to believe you and no one will. You tell your girlfriend and she does not believe you. She thinks you probably did something to provoke them. She wonders about your sexuality. She asks you if you enjoyed it. You know now that you cannot ever tell your parents. Your mother might understand but not your father, he would never believe you. He would definitely believe you were a homosexual...No! You can never tell your parents!

Your pain does not end there — you have difficulty sleeping nights and the guys that raped you call you from time to time to ask you "if you want some more of what you got!" You become afraid of seeing them so you do not go out of your apartment unless you have to. You decide not to prosecute the rape because the prosecutor's office tells you that because you had several drinks with them, it would appear that you were "asking for it." Somehow the word has gotten around campus that you are gay and all of your friends start avoiding you as if you had AIDS. You feel like you are all alone.

No one understands the pain and humiliation that you are going through and for the first time in your life, you contemplate suicide. If only someone would believe you.

Then one day a woman comes up to you. She is from the Women's Support Group on campus. You know her, but not too well. She says she would like to talk to you. You are reluctant but she confides that, like you, she too was a victim of rape. She gets you in touch with the Rape Crisis Center counselor. You join a support group of other male rape victims and for the first time since the assault, you know you are not alone. You know that you are not the only victim of rape.

Does this sound impossible? When a man has been in a Federal Penitentiary for 15 to 20 years, it may not make any difference to him anymore. He may "do it to you" just to humiliate you. Remember, rape is a crime of power, not sex, so whether you are a male or female, it can happen to you too!

Rape – Date Rape – Sexual Assault – is a crime of power, not sex. The primary reason for rape is to gain power and control over another person. A rapist often feels that if he can dominate another person, he will somehow feel better about himself. In other words, he rapes to increase his self esteem. He feels that he is so worthless and out of control that the only way he can feel in control and on top again to assault, degrade, humiliate, dominate and rape another person.

When you think of rape, maybe now you will think of some of the incredible trauma that a rape victim undergoes for years after the assault. How much more horror would it be for you if the guys that raped you were your friends—men that you knew and trusted?

Can you imagine other people accusing you of "making up the rape to get even with the guys?" Can you imagine going through all of the humiliation unless it actually occurred? So you can see, anybody who claims a woman is inventing a rape or sexual assault to get even or to get attention does not know what he or she is talking about.

For thousands of years men have been manipulating, controlling, abusing and raping women. These rapists were often not crazed maniacs but people like you and me who felt they had the right to take the body of a woman and use it for their own purpose regardless of her will. (Read *Against Our Will* by Susan Brownmiller.)

We must not only stop raping women, we must change the way we look at women, think about women, talk about women and act with women. We must also start raising our sons to respect their sisters, other girls and all women as they grow up.

Rape does not start with the physical act of rape. It starts in our minds, our words, our attitudes about women, and it ends in violent degradation.

Every woman is not a rape victim, but every woman is the "potential" victim of a rape.

Not every man is a rapist, but *every man* is a "potential" rapist and it starts in your mind.

Think about it!!!

If you can reprogram your mind to get ahead in the business world or in athletics and consciously turn your life into a success through your thoughts, then you can also change your thoughts about women, if you really want to.

* Think about these statements:

1) Having sex does not make you a man!

2) Manipulating a woman does not make you a man!

3) "Scoring" is something you do in athletics—it has no place in a relationship!

4) A relationship is *not* a game where you win or lose!

5) A date is not a contest of wills!

6) Asking a woman if she is interested in having sex with you before you proceed does not make you a wimp!

7) Respecting a woman's wishes in regards to sex is the safe thing to do!

8) Anything short of mutual consent in a sexual encounter is beneath you and can be considered rape!

9) The physical, moral, legal and long term consequences of forcing sex from a woman can ruin her life and also yours.

10) You owe it to yourself to clarify her consent before you assume she wants to have sex. Silence is not consent—silence is NO. After she says no, it's rape!!!

"Rape is a man's problem. It is men who rape and men who collectively have the power to end rape. This will only begin to happen when men cease blaming women for rape."
—From *Men On Rape*
By Timothy Beneke

What can a man do to prevent rape?
Contribute to a Rape Crisis Center. There is nothing more enlightening to a man than to see the consequences of men's anger against women. Join or start an "anti-rape" men's support group.

Can a woman be raped by her own husband? **Yes.** No matter what the circumstances, no matter what the relationship of the man to the woman, **forced sex is rape!**

Send for more information from:

RAVEN (Rape And Violence End Now)
P.O. Box 24159
St. Louis, MO 63190

NCOMR (National Clearing House On Marital and Date Rape)
Women's History Research Center
2325 Oak Street
Berkeley, CA 94708
Phone (415) 548-1770

**REMEMBER – AGAINST THE WILL
IS AGAINST THE LAW !!!**

> "The greatest thing in this world is not so much where we are, but in what direction we are moving."
>
> Oliver Wendell Holmes

Chapter Twelve: Caring Words and Recommendations

TO HER SIGNIFICANT OTHER:

Rape is a crime that has many victims—not only the actual person who was raped, but also friends, lovers, family and anyone who is currently in a relationship with her or the man who committed the crime. The significant others' response to her after the rape can be the most important factor in her healing. You will feel many of the same feelings that she is going through but your reactions will not be as intense as her feelings.

Guilt: It is common for you to feel guilty for not being there to protect her.

Anger: Obviously you will be angry at the rapist, but taking the law into you own hands and rushing out to "get the ____" is not what she needs right now. She has enough to worry about without wondering if you are going to get killed or put in jail. Also your rage against the rapist may be interpreted by her as anger/violence against her as well.

Depression: You, like she, may get depressed at the incident because it has changed both of your lives forever. She may withdraw from you and seem to change. This is normal. You may want your relationship to go back to normal as quickly as possible…this is unrealistic and unfair. It also places blame upon her because she can't get beyond the incident according to your time schedule. **GIVE HER TIME.**

Denial: You may react by pointing out that she did not get hurt so why can't she just forget about it? This attempt to minimize her pain will only make her more isolated from you and the world, as well as telling her that you really do not understand what she is going through. She needs to talk about it. Let her.

Disbelief: You may not believe her 100%. Maybe she did not act the way you think she should have or maybe she was not physically beaten to the degree that there are bruises. If you do not believe her it will only harm her. She needs your **unconditional support** right now. Do not hold back. If you have trouble understanding her, her story and the way she's reacting to you, contact the Rape Crisis counselor. She can give you some insight into her condition.

Overprotection: You may want to take control of her life, never leave her alone, etc. Remember, she has just gone through a life threatening situation in which her control was taken away from her. She needs to feel that you will protect her but will also encourage her to take control of her own life again.

What to do...What she needs from you:

(1) Believe her: regardless of the circumstances. If she feels like she has been raped, then she has. Do not question her. Even if her story does not make sense, remember she has just been through a life-threatening situation and that is bound to have an impact on her.

(2) Reassure her: She needs to know that what she is feeling is normal for someone who has been raped. She is bound to have a myriad of confusing feelings right now. Tell her it's okay, that it's going to take time for her to recover. Express some of your own feelings as well. It will give her permission to share what she is feeling too.

(4) Be there to listen: Listen to her and hear what she is really saying about herself. Do not close the door on what has happened before she is ready. Every rape victim responds differently to the assault and recovery time varies. Trying to minimize the attack's impact on her will isolate her and drive her away from you. **Be patient.**

(5) Let her know how you feel: Share your feelings with her as well as with a Rape Crisis counselor or therapist...you will need help too. Don't tell her "I understand" or "I know how you feel" unless you have been a victim or rape yourself. You can't know how she feels or what she is going through—just listen and be there.

(6) Don't take control: It is normal to want to rescue her, to protect her, to surround her with your presence. Be patient. Reassure her that you will be there as much as she needs but that you know that she is capable of making decisions and being in control of her own life. Besides, you can't be there all the time for her anyway and this only encourages her dependence on you. It is okay for her to be dependent on you for a while but her independence should always be encouraged.

(7) Patience, patience, patience: Don't expect too much from her. Her ability to recover and the length of time it will take depends on you, her family, the kind of help she gets, and her self esteem prior to the rape. Understand that if your sexual relationship changes, this is normal. She may take her anger out on you and on a subconscious or conscious level put you in the same category as the rapist. She may feel that all men are the same. Keep telling her "I'm on your side" and "I know you're angry—I'm angry too." Encourage her to get professional help and even agree to get help with her. I know you were not the one who was raped, but you both need help to deal with the stress of the rape on your relationship. And there is nothing wrong with getting help for yourself either with a Rape Crisis counselor, psychologist, etc., because you may need professional help too.

1. Remember the journey from pain takes time.
2. The journey involves releasing fears.
3. She can grow in spite of her pain if she gets support.

4. Give her what she needs.
5. Be patient with her moods; never give up on her.
6. Tell her you will be there when she needs you.
7. Accept her own unique way of dealing with her trauma.
8. Ultimately this experience can be used as a means to change her life for the better, depending on how she looks at it, but for now allow her the time to heal without your time limits or your expectations.
9. You, like her, have been victimized by rape. Give yourself time to heal as well. Be honest in your own needs and avoid denial as it only leads to emotional blocks.
10. You may need professional help also in order to understand and cope with the aftermath of rape. Getting help does not make you less of a man. It means you have the courage to know when an objective viewpoint is needed.

What can universities, colleges and women's groups do to prevent date rape?

Universities and colleges have a responsibility to be honest with their students and parents about crime and acquaintance or date rape on and off campus. The resulting legal liabilities for hiding potential dangers can lead to law suits from students and the families of victims. It can also, of course, be devastating to enrollment and reputation. Education is always the first step in changing behavior.

Several states have passed laws requiring schools to report crime data to freshmen students and their families. And, as of this writing, Congressman Bill Goodling has introduced The Crime Awareness and Security Information Act (H.R. 3344) that would require all colleges and universities to report campus crime to the general public and the F.B.I.

FIVE RECOMMENDATIONS:

(1) Identifying the dangerous areas and conditions that often contribute to date rape is imperative. Publicize the school's stand on date rape and the consequences involved for perpetrators.

(2) The education of women and men as to the dynamics of dating and date rape is imperative. Establish ongoing attitude-awareness groups to keep the issue at the forefront of campus concerns.

(3) Establish a highly publicized step-by-step procedure for victims of rape - what to do and where to report as well as victim support groups. Put information (like this book) in new student orientation packets.

(4) Communicate that you care. Tell women that you believe them and then follow through with the needed support.

(5) Women's groups can set up something similar to the Better Business Bureau. If you are familiar with the BBB, a consumer can call the BBB to find out if there is a complaint file or report on a particular business before they decide whether to do business with them or not. The BBB looks into it's files and makes a report to the consumer that X business has had X complaints about it. So a woman's group can have a complaint procedure for reporting men who rape their dates. A woman would come to the support group to report a man who raped her. The group would then take down the information as to what happened, when and where and put it into the files under the man's name.

When new female students come to the university, they can call the support group and check to see whether their proposed date has a history of violence on dates. This can be especially important if the woman does not feel she can report it to the police or even campus security. This process also puts her in touch with other women who will have a tendency to be supportive and to believe her. Each school can have requirements that minimize false reporting but it is important to believe women first. Validation can come later.

It is also important to have a record system that identifies men who rape before they can rape again. The records, if properly maintained, can have a preventative effect on men's behavior. If a man can't get a date (or at least can't get a vulnerable date,) then maybe he or his friends will be less likely to destroy their own reputations on campus by any further acts of violence.

Is it possible that women would smear a man's reputation when there has been no crime committed? Yes, anything is possible, however for years men have been all too ready to slander a woman's reputation by saying that "she's an easy lay!" even when it wasn't true.

> *"Life must be lived forwards, but can only be understood backwards."*
> Kierkegaard

Chapter Thirteen: Self Defense – Martial Arts, Weapons, What Works and What's Realistic?

A word of caution: According to the law, in defending yourself, you can use force only of sufficient intensity to repel your attacker. Excessive force could result in being prosecuted on criminal charges.

In essence, what this means is that you have every right to defend yourself if you use about the same force as your attacker. If he pushes you around and you kill him with a gun, then you have used excessive force to repel him. This is most common when people use lethal weapons to defend themselves.

The best defense is your own awareness. It costs you nothing and will always be there when you need it. Listen to your instincts—they have saved many people from imminent danger. The more you listen to that "inner voice" the stronger it gets.

Should you enroll in a self defense course or martial arts? Yes, if you have the time and can commit to a long-term training in survival skills. If you think that you can learn how to successfully defend yourself from a violent assault by taking a couple of classes in martial arts, you are misleading yourself. Talk to a certified instructor and you will find it takes years of training in order to be really successful. Understand that training for competition in a classroom setting and defending your life on the street are two different situations. Criminals do not play by the rules. They may do the most unexpected things to throw you off guard.

One of the most unusual and seemingly successful self defense programs is taught by Matt Thomas in San Fransico, California and is called **Model Mugging.** Sounds like a course in attacking mannequins, doesn't it? Actually, "Model Mugging is a highly specialized self defense course for women which provides training that teaches women to change a "freeze response" to an action response. Women learn that they can channel adrenaline, the body's natural response to fear and danger, into effective, reflexive, full contact fighting skills." (This quote is taken from *Model Mugging News,* September 1988.)

The Bay area Model Mugging Program has two basic levels. Level 1 is knockout defense against a single unarmed assailant. (This is the standard MM course.) Level 2 picks up where the first class ends and includes an introduction to weapons. There will be more muggings, technique review, video review, use of impact meter and an introduction to weapons in which the students learn the fundamentals of street fighting. Thomas is a black belt in Karate, Judo, and Japanese Fencing and has graduated from Stanford University. The Model Mugging Course in the San Francisco area can be reached by calling (408) 647-2204.

Model Mugging Chapters:

Boston, MA	(617) 482-4071
Chicago, IL	(312) 338-4545
Kansas City, MO	(816) 931-8022
Honolulu, HI	(808) 949-5525
Los Angeles, CA	(800) 541-KICK
Monterey, CA	(408) 646-KICK
Boulder, CO	(303) 442-1068
San Fransico, CA	(415) 342-BAMM
San Luis Obispo, CA	(805) 544-KICK
Santa Barbara, CA	(805) 684-8228

Santa Cruz, CA   (408) 429-1560

All other inquiries call (408) 647-2004

Model Mugging
P.O. Box 921
Monterey, CA 93942

Using Common Ordinary Items as Weapons of Self Defense:

There is a lot of misinformation that has been disseminated in regards to self defense. **Remember that the only way that self defense works is to incapacitate your attacker long enough to escape.**

List of readily available non-lethal weapons
(These can be dangerous if used in a stranger rape situation, because of the likelihood of increased violence that often accompanies the assault.)

Hat Pins	(go for face, eyes)
Plastic Lemons	(spray in eyes)
Lighted Cigarettes	(burn his face, hands, arms)
Umbrella	(jab the point into his stomach, groin)
Magazine or Newspaper	(Strike across bridge of nose)
Hard Bound Book	(strike across nose)
Forks	(stab it in his face)
Rat Tailed Comb	(stab it into his eyes)
Pen, Pencil, Nail File	(jab into his face or eyes)
Pocketbook	(hit him several times in the face)
Keys	(scrape him across the face)

117

*These weapons can be totally useless or can inflict permanent damage to the attacker. If you feel you can't take the risk of permanently harming your attacker, then use a non lethal weapon. These can also cause you more damage, because if they do not incapacitate him, he may become more angry which will turn him violently against you.

These easily obtainable items may not do sufficient damage to incapacitate him. They may however be more effective in a Date Rape situation. Since date rapists are more interested in having sex with the victim, they do not tend to be as violent as stranger rapists. However, there are always exceptions.

Common Physical Self Defense Maneuvers:

1) The open hand blow or karate chop to the side of the neck.
2) Karate chop to the nose.
3) Biting him as hard as you can.
4) Karate chop under the nose.
5) The open hand stab to the throat.
6) Heel of the palm thrust under the chin.
7) Heel of the palm thrust up under the nose.
8) Elbow to rib cage, stomach.
9) Kick him in the shins.
10) Kick him at the kneecap.
11) Stomp on his foot with your high heels.
12) Grab his little finger, bend it back and break it.
13) A kick to the groin should be the second target since he will protect himself there first.

I have refrained from including specifics or illustrations of these maneuvers because they should never be tried unless they have been practiced as part of a self defense course with qualified instructors. Understand that practice is important - just learning the right moves does not mean you can commit to pulling out the stops and inflict damage to your attacker. **To stop an attacker, you have to be willing to hurt him and hurt him bad!!!** Remember, he does not care whether he hurts you or not - he does not care, period. To use any self defense training effectively, you have to be just as uncaring about his welfare as he is about yours.

Pulling Out the Stops

Whatever you decide to do if and when sexual assault happens to you (Recent statistics have also indicated that one out of four college women will be assaulted before she gets out of school.), you must be ready to defend your life with all the power you can summon. Taking self defense courses is a good idea if they are available in your area and if you can commit the time and energy to them.

In the meantime, while you are taking the self defense courses or if you are not able to commit to the time, energy or financial costs of a particular training program, you might want to consider a more sophisticated non-lethal weapon, especially if you do not want to risk permanent injury to your attacker.

Non Lethal Weapons

"For the protection of themselves, their family, their property and their communities, citizens must be encouraged to seek out non-lethal forms of protection."
—The Presidential Commission on Crime and Justice, 1984-85

I believe in non-lethal weapons. The best, most deadly weapon in the world is of no use to you if you cannot bring yourself to use it. **Hesitation kills!** Whatever you carry, you have to be able to use it almost without thinking at a moment's notice. You do not have time to stop and leisurely consider the ramifications if you use it on someone who actually meant you no harm.

The ideal non-lethal device or weapon can be used without the worry that if you made a mistake, it will come back to haunt you, causing permanent injury or death to your attacker. It should interrupt the assault long enough for you to escape, and incapacitate him temporarily causing no permanent damage or side effects.

Since most date rape situations do not contain excessive violence against the victim and depend upon the attacker's size and weight to gain control of the woman (most date rapists do not use a lethal weapon on their victims), the use of a non-lethal weapon can tip the scales in a woman's favor.

Stun Guns: There are several different varieties, but the most common is a hand-held unit that carries 50,000 volts. They are powered by a nickle-cadmium battery (rechargeable but expensive) or a standard alkaline battery (non-rechargeable). The battery chargers will cost you about $12.00 to $15.00. The stun gun can incapacitate an attacker for several minutes. The drawbacks are that the entire unit is somewhat expensive. Traditionally a 50,000 watt stun gun will cost you approximately $59.95 to $79.95. This is a "contact device," that is, in order to incapacitate the attacker, you must be close enough to touch him and hold the stun gun on your attacker for 3–5 minutes. If you are close enough to touch him he is also close enough to touch you. Stun guns have also been used to torture the victims when the criminals have taken these devices away from them.

Mace or **Tear Gas:** Most people think of Mace when they think of tear gas. I do not recommend Mace/C.N., because it does not work the same on all people. The label tells you to "use extreme care with intoxicated, drugged, demented, enraged or other persons having reduced sensitivity to pain and who may react with violence if not incapacitated with this weapon." **Tear Gas and Mace are not the same.** I carry tear gas. I have given crime prevention seminars for over six years and spoken to over 250,000 people. From the research that I have done, it seems to be the best alternative for the average person.

(1) A good tear gas (CS, 1% Orthochlorobenzalmalononitrile) can incapacitate an attacker long enough for the victim of the assault to escape.

(2) Tear gas can spray from 3 - 10 feet and can incapacitate from a distance before the attacker makes physical contact with the intended victim.

(3) Many people, especially women, are uncomfortable with carrying a lethal weapon (gun, knife) and would hesitate before using it on an attacker. A non-lethal weapon like tear gas is often used without hesitation because a woman is reassured that she will not cause permanent injury or death to her attacker.

(4) The antidote for a good tear gas is water and fresh air. Use no oils, creams or salves. The effects will wear off in approximately 30 - 45 minutes.

(5) Look for a tear gas that contains an ultraviolet dye in it. This marks the assailant for identification purposes. This dye tends to wear off in approximately 48 hours.

Like any device, the selection of a good tear gas is imperative. Do not purchase from a retail store as tear gas expires in one (1) year. Not all tear gases are the same. Some are not only ineffective, they are also undependable. **Get tear gas only from a manufacturer.** Retail merchants including pawn shops, and police supply stores often keep products on the shelf for many years causing your tear gas to become useless. Tear gas is a class #3 weapon. In most states, it is legal to use it in the defense of your life or property. Check your local police departments for laws pertaining to tear gas. Indiscriminate or unwarranted use, however, can lead to arrest.

Do not carry tear gas aboard an aircraft or through security checkpoints. It is illegal to do so and it will be confiscated.

Drawbacks:

Blowback: As with any spray, blowback is possible. Wind speed and weather conditions may affect the dispersal of the chemical.

Expired Chemicals: Tear gas **must** be test fired immediately upon purchase and every 90 days thereafter. Check the date of manufacture. Shake the canister frequently to see if the liquid has dried up. Despite what some manufacturers claim, no tear gas will be 100% effective after one year from the date of its manufacture.

AIR HORNS & Noise Makers: Whistles, air horns, etc. can also be effective in date rape situations.

Air horns are often the best idea and are recommended by Jack MacLean (The Superthief) in his book *The Secrets of a Superthief.*

Criminals hate loud noises, because noise attracts attention. I recommend air horns. They are small cans of pressurized freon with a plastic horn on top. When a woman pushes the button, the loud blast can be heard for up to 1 mile. **AIR HORNS SCARE THE CRIMINAL AND SUMMON HELP AT THE SAME TIME.**

"No weapon is a panacea for all situations and all crimes." Use your head, follow your instincts, take self defense classes, and above all listen to that small voice inside of you that can tell you something is wrong. If you feel uncomfortable with the guy or his friends, get out of there at once. The only thing that you can always depend on is your mind. Use it!!!

Afterword:

This book will, I hope, have an impact on the dating habits and relationships of young people as well as all people that date. It is important to remember that although this book is primarily about Date Rape, Acquaintance Rape is also a significant problem. Anyone can be raped by anyone else. You are more vulnerable to people you know and spend time with, simply because your guard is down around those you trust. Does this mean that you shouldn't trust anyone? No, but it does mean that **anyone can become untrustworthy**; your date, your doctor, your pastor, your friend, your husband, or even your father. Trust your feelings.

You don't have to go out with "him," if you feel uncomfortable with his behavior, or if that inner voice tells you he could be dangerous.

YOU HAVE CHOICES!!!

You don't have to drink alcohol, or get drunk to be accepted. No matter how much pressure you feel to "go along" and do what everyone else is doing...it is still your choice, and your's alone.

YOU HAVE CHOICES!!!

You don't have to go to bed with him. Young men feel a tremendous amout of peer pressure to "prove themselves" to their friends and be a MAN. At their age, the most common way to feel like a man is to get laid. He may feel that he needs it, that he'll be in pain if you don't have sex with him, that you owe it to him, or that everybody's doing it. If he feels inadequate because you don't sleep with him, then that's "his problem" not yours.

YOU HAVE CHOICES!!!

Rape is the ultimate violation, because it takes away a woman's right to choose her sexual partner, or whether she wants to participate in this very intimate act at all. Forced sex is rape! Unconscious sex is rape! And even if Date or Acquaintance Rape happens to you, please understand that you still have choices. You have the choice of whether you report the crime.. You have the choice of whether you get a medical exam. You have the choice of whether you prosecute your attacker, and you also have the choice of whether you get help and contact a Rape Crisis Center counselor. I hope this book will help you make the "right choices," both before, during and after the crime, if and when it happens.

Remember **YOU ARE NOT ALONE.**

Before He Takes You Out
(The Safe Dating Guide for the 90's)

Fifteen Ways to Prevent Date or Acquaintance Rape

1. Communicate up front with him.
2. Be assertive with him about sex—"he" can't read your mind.
3. If you want a platonic (non-sexual) relationship, say so.
4. If there is to be no sex tonight, say so.
5. Introduce him to your roommate before you go out. Tell your roommate where you are going and when you will return.
6. If this is your first date with him, meet him for lunch and take your own car.
7. Remember, isolated spots can be dangerous. Meet him in public and stay around other people until you are sure he is safe.
8. Fraternity "rush" parties can be dangerous. Pour your own drinks and watch out for upstairs bedrooms or basements.
9. Alcohol and drugs are tools of date rapists. Getting high or drunk will make his job easier and your escape more difficult.
10. Do not let him intimidate you. If you feel uncomfortable with him, get out of there and always trust your instincts.
11. Always carry a telephone emergency card and enough cash to take a car home if you have to get away from him.
12. Never leave a bar or party with a guy you do not know yet.
13. Take a self defense course such as "model mugging" or martial arts.
14. Carry an air horn to alert others to your emergency and scare him.
15. You may also wish to carry a "non-lethal" weapon such as tear gas, but if you do, do not be afraid to use it.

If it Happens to You

1. Get to safety (Get away from him.)
2. Don't wash or change
   (This may destroy evidence.)
3. Report the crime
   (Call the Police or Campus Security.)
4. Get a medical exam
   (Your rape crisis center will help.)
5. Call someone to be with you
   (Someone you can trust.)
6. Contact a rape crisis center
   (They understand and care.)
7. Ask someone to stay with you
   (Do not be alone, now.)
8. Get into counseling
   (You will need a support group.)
9. Be gentle on yourself (Recovery takes time.)
10. Do not minimize the assault
    (Rape is a violent crime.)
11. Remember—it was not your fault!!!

It's Not Your Fault

No matter how stupid you feel...
No matter if you knew the guy...
No matter if you were drunk or high...
No matter if you had sex with him before...
No matter how popular he is on campus...
No matter if you said yes, then said no...
No matter if no one believes you were raped...
No matter if you decide not to report him...
No matter what happened, it is not your fault and it does not change the fact that you were raped.

Rape is an act of violence, not an act of sex!
Rape is a "life threatening situation"—whatever you did to escape, your first priority, then and now, is to save your life!

Rape Crisis Centers in the U.S.

The following list was compiled from the National Directory of Rape Prevention and Treatment Resources (National Institute of Mental Health). Check with your local police department for listings in your area or with "directory information" for phone numbers. Check under RAPE.

Alabama
Birmingham
(205) 323-7273

Montgomery
(205) 263-4481

Tuscaloosa
(205) 345-1600

Alaska
Anchorage
(907) 276-7273
(907) 277-0222

Fairbanks
(907) 452-7273
(907) 452-2293

Nome
(907) 443-5444

Arizona
Phoenix
(602) 255-3609

Tucson
(602) 792-8021

Arkansas
Fort Smith
(501) 452-6650

Little Rock
(501) 375-5181

California
Bakersfield
(805) 861-2251

Berkeley
(415) 548-4343

Chico
(916) 342-7273

Claremont
(714) 626-4357

California (Cont.)

Concord
(415) 798-7273
(415) 798-4575

Fairfield
(707) 422-7273

Fresno
(209) 222-7273
(209) 486-4692

Laguna Beach
(714) 494-0761

Long Beach
(213) 597-2002
(213) 388-0446 (Asian)

Merced
(209) 383-2818

Oakland
(415) 655-8988

Palo Alto
(415) 493-7273
(415) 494-0972

Pasadena
(213) 973-3385

Riverside
(714) 686-7273

San Bernardino
(714) 882-5291

San Francisco
(415) 647-7273
(415) 558-3824

Davis
(916) 758-8400
(916) 662-1133
(916) 371-1907

Fort Bragg
(707) 964-4357

Goleta
(805) 963-1696

Lompoc
(805) 736-8913

Los Angeles
(213) 262-0944 (bilingual)

Monterey
(213) 375-4357

Orange
(714) 831-9110

Paramount
(213) 868-3783

Placentia
(714) 524-5040

Sacramento
(916) 447-7273

San Diego
(714) 436-7137

San Jose
(408) 287-3000
(408) 277-2262

California (Cont.)

San Luis Obispo
(805) 549-5800

San Mateo
(415) 349-7273

San Rafael
(415) 924-2100

Santa Cruz
(408) 426-7273

Santa Rosa
(707) 545-7273
(707) 545-7270

San Luis Rey
(714) 757-3500

San Pablo
(415) 236-7273

Santa Barbara
(805) 966-9762 (bilingual)

Santa Monica
(213) 451-1511

Stockton
(209) 465-4997

Colorado

Aspen
(303) 925-5400

Colorado Springs
(303) 471-4357
(303) 633-4601

Durango
(303) 259-1110

Greeley
(303) 352-4551

Boulder
(303) 441-3730

Denver
(303) 893-6000

Fort Collins
(303) 493-3888

Grand Junction
(303) 243-0190

Connecticut

Bridgeport
(203) 333-2233

Middletown
(203) 346-7233

Hartford
(203) 525-1163

Milford
(203) 878-1212

Connecticut (Cont.)

New Haven
(203) 624-2273

Stamford
(203) 329-2929
(203) 348-9346

New London
(203) 442-4357

Storrs
(203) 423-9595

Waterbury
(203) 753-3613

Delaware

Newark
(302) 738-2226

Wilmington
(302) 658-5011

District of Columbia
(202) 628-3228
(202) 543-5580
(202) 727-4906

Florida

Gainesville
(904) 377-6888

Jacksonville
(904) 354-3114

Ocala
(904) 622-8495

Pensacola
(904) 433-7273

Tampa
(813) 251-8629

Hollywood
(305) 963-6040

Miami
(305) 325-6949
(305) 358-4357

Orlando
(305) 841-5111

Sarasota
(813) 365-1976

West Palm Beach
(305) 833-7273

Georgia

Albany
(912) 432-7273

Athens
(404) 353-1912

Georgia (Cont.)

Atlanta
(404) 589-4861
(404) 659-7273
(404) 894-6635
(404) 892-3476

Brunswick
(912) 267-0760

Dalton
(404) 259-2305

Dublin
(912) 275-1613

Gainesville
(404) 535-8962

Hinesville
(912) 767-3863

Macon
(912) 746-1551
(912) 746-0531

Milledgeville
(912) 453-4891

Savannah
(912) 233-7273

Stockbridge
(404) 389-2266

Warner Robbins
(912) 922-4144
(912) 922-0949

Augusta
(404) 724-5200
(404) 722-9011
(Beeper # 966)

Carrollton
(404) 834-3326

Decatur
(404) 377-5365

Duluth
(404) 497-0408

Griffin
(404) 229-8303

Lawrenceville
(404) 962-1618

Marietta
(404) 428-2666

Riverdale
(404) 471-4357
(404) 991-8512

Statesboro
(912) 764-6234

Valdosta
(912) 333-5157

Hawaii
(808) 737-5465
(808) 524-7273
(808) 247-2148

Idaho
Boise
(208) 345-7273

Caldwell
(208) 454-0421

Nampa
(208) 467-7112

Rupert
(208) 436-3406

Burley
(208) 454-0421

Moscow
(208) 885-6616 (8AM - 5PM)
(208) 882-4511 (nights)

Pocatello
(208) 232-9169

Twin Falls
(208) 734-7273

Illinois
Aurora
(312) 897-1003

Canton
(309) 647-2466

Chicago
(312) 372-6600
(312) 762-0377
(312) 947-5140
(312) 947-6735
(312) 942-5000
(312) 883-5688
(312) 528-3303
(312) 583-4050 (ext. 375/376)

East St. Louis
(618) 692-2197

Evanston
(312) 492-6500

Belleville
(618) 397-0963

Champaign
(217) 337-2533

Danville
(217) 442-4466

Decatur
(217) 429-7444

Dupage
(309) 755-3428

Edwardsville
(618) 692-2197

Granite City
(618) 451-5722

Illinois (Cont.)

Joliet
(815) 722-3344

Rockford
(815) 964-4044

Springfield
(217) 785-2080

Lombard
(312) 495-3927

Rock Island
(309) 793-1000

Indiana

Columbus
(812) 376-7273

Fort Wayne
(219) 426-7273
(219) 482-9111

Indianapolis
(317) 788-9506
(317) 353-5947
(317) 353-5931
(317) 630-7791

Unionville
(812) 339-3110

Warsaw
(219) 267-7169
(317) 545-1116

Evansville
(812) 425-4355

Gary
(219) 937-0450
(219) 980-4207
(219) 769-3141

Lawrenceburg
(812) 537-1302

South Bend
(219) 232-3344

Vincennes
(812) 885-3291

Iowa

Ames
(515) 292-1101

Davenport
(319) 326-9191

Iowa City
(319) 338-4800

Cedar Rapids
(319) 398-3955
(319) 365-1458

Fort Dodge
(515) 573-8000

Kansas

Hays
(913) 628-1041

Hutchinson
(316) 663-2522

Lawrence
(913) 841-2345

Topeka
(913) 295-8499

Humboldt
(316) 473-2241

Junction City
(913) 238-4131

Manhattan
(913) 532-6432

Wichita
(316) 685-0201

Kentucky

Ashland
(606) 324-1141

Frankfurt
(502) 564-4448

Lexington
(606) 253-2511

Newport
(606) 491-3335

Corbin
(606) 528-7010

Harlan
(606) 573-1624

Louisville
(502) 459-5166

Louisiana

Alexandra
(318) 445-4357

New Orleans
(504) 821-6000, 586-4061

Baton Rouge
(504) 389-3456

Shreveport
(318) 222-0556

Maine

Portland
(207) 774-3613

Maryland

Annapolis
(301) 263-0330

Baltimore
(301) 366-7273, 383-5608

Bethesda
(301) 656-9449

Cheverly
(301) 341-4942

College Park
(301) 454-4616

Columbia
(301) 997-3292

Edgewater
(301) 956-4200

Gaithersburg
(301) 948-0922

Massachusetts

Amherst
(413) 545-0800

Boston
(617) 482-3663

Cambridge
(617) 482-0329, 492-7273
(617) 492-7273

Dedham
(617) 326-1600

Hyannis
(617) 771-1080

Lynn
(617) 595-7273

Newton
(617) 964-2800

Northhampton
(413) 586-5555

Springfield
(413) 781-8100

Worcester
(617) 799-5700

Michigan

Ann Arbor
(313) 994-1616

Bay City
(517) 893-4551

Detroit
(313) 227-4487 Days
(313) 224-0550 Nights

East Lansing
(517) 337-1717

Grand Rapids
(616) 774-3535

Kalamazoo
(616) 383-6386

Michigan (Cont.)

Muskegon
(616) 722-3333

Port Huron
(313) 985-7161

Pontiac
(313) 332-4357

Saginaw
(517) 755-6565

Minnesota

Alexandria
(612) 763-6638

Brainerd
(218) 828-1216

Fairmont
(507) 235-3456

Minneapolis
(612) 871-2603
(617) 825-4357

St. Cloud
(612) 251-4357

Winona
(507) 452-4440

Austin
(507) 437-6680

Duluth
(218) 727-4353

Grand Rapids
(218) 326-1034

Northfield
(507) 645-5555

Rochester
(507) 289-0636

St. Paul
(612) 296-7080

Woodbury
(612) 738-3600

Mississippi

Hattiesburg
(601) 266-4100

Columbia
(314) 442-3322

Kansas City
(816) 932-2171

Jackson
(601) 354-1113

Jefferson City
(314) 751-3448

St. Joseph
(816) 233-7510

Missouri (Cont.)
St. Louis
(314) 531-2597

Springfield
(417) 866-1969

Montana
Billings
(406) 259-6506

Helena
(406) 443-5353

Kalispell
(406) 755-5067

Missoula
(406) 543-7606

Nebraska
Lincoln
(402) 471-2039
(402) 471-2144

Omaha
(402) 345-7273

Nevada
Las Vegas
(702) 735-1111
(702) 386-4204

New Hampshire
Concord
(800) 852-3311

Lebanon
(603) 448-4400

Manchester
(603) 668-2299

Nashua
(603) 883-3044

Portsmouth
(603) 436-2145

New Jersey
Annandale
(201) 782-4357

Atlantic City
(609) 345-6700

New Jersey (Cont.)

East Orange
(201) 672-9685

Flemington
(201) 733-7273

Moorestown
(609) 234-8888

Newark
(201) 733-7273

Somerville
(201) 526-4100

Elizabeth
(201) 654-3000

Hackensack
(201) 488-0400

New Brunswick
(201) 828-7273

Plainfield
(201) 668-2000

Trenton
(609) 984-6347

New Mexico

Alamagordo
(505) 437-8680

Artesia
(505) 746-9042

Deming
(505) 546-2174

Gallup
(505) 722-5200

Las Cruces
(505) 526-3371

Los Alamos
(505) 662-7600

Roswell
(505) 622-7600

Taos
(505) 758-2910

Albuquerque
(505) 247-0707, 277-3716

Carlsbad
(505) 885-8888

Farmington
(505) 325-1906

Hobbs
(505) 393-6633

Las Vegas
(505) 425-6794

Portales
(800) 432-2159

Santa Fe
(505) 982-4667

Tucumari
(505) 461-3013

New York

Binghamton
(607) 722-4256

Brooklyn
(212) 735-2424

Jamaica
(212) 990-3187

Niagara Falls
(716) 278-4528

Oneonta
(607) 432-2115

Rochester
(716) 546-2595

Schenectady
(518) 346-2266

White Plains
(914) 592-8400

Bronx
(212) 579-5326

Buffalo
(716) 838-5980

New York City
(212) 870-1875
(212) 790-8068
(212) 233-3000
(212) 577-7777

Oceanside
(516) 764-2600

Plattsburgh
(518) 563-6904

Sanborn
(716) 731-3595

Syracuse
(315) 474-7011

North Carolina

Asheville
(704) 255-7576

Chapel Hill
(919) 967-7273

Concord
(704) 788-1130

Greensboro
(919) 273-7273

Burlington
(919) 227-6220

Charlotte
(704) 373-0982

Durham
(919) 688-4353

Greenville
(919) 752-7151

North Carolina (Cont.)
High Point
(919) 431-7273

Statesville
(704) 872-3403

Salisbury
(704) 636-9222

Winston Salem
(919) 723-5494
(919) 724-7911

North Dakota
Fargo
(701) 293-7273

Grand Forks
(701) 746-6666

Ohio
Akron
(216) 434-7273

Cincinnati
(513) 381-5610

Columbus
(614) 221-4447

Toledo
(419) 385-5768

Canton
(216) 452-9911

Cleveland
(216) 431-7774

Dayton
(513) 254-8406

Warren
(216) 393-1565

Oklahoma
Enid
(405) 234-1111

Oklahoma City
(405) 521-0234
(405) 524-7273

Norman
(405) 321-1444

Oregon
Corvalis
(503) 754-0110

Oregon City
(503) 655-8616

Eugene
(503) 687-4478

Portland
(503) 248-5059

Oregon (Cont.)
Salem
(503) 399-7722

Pennsylvania
Allentown
(215) 437-6610

Butler
(412) 282-4153
(412) 287-0791

Doylestown
(215) 348-2911

East Stroudsburg
(717) 421-4000

Greensburg
(412) 836-1122

Johnstown
(814) 536-5361

Meadville
(814) 724-2732

Norristown
(215) 278-3429

Pittsburgh
(412) 355-5764,
(412) 661-6066
(412) 765-2731

Scranton
(717) 346-4671

Uniontown
(412) 437-3737

Altoona
(814) 946-2141

Chambersburg
(717) 264-4444

Du Bois
(814) 371-1100

Erie
(814) 456-1001

Harrisburg
(717) 238-7273

Lancaster
(717) 392-7358

Media
(215) 566-4342

Philadelphia
(215) 922-3434
(215) 568-6627

Reading
(215) 372-7273

Rochester
(412) 775-0131

State College
(814) 234-5050

Pennsylvania (Cont.)

West Chester
(215) 692-7273

Wilkes-Barre
(717) 823-0765

Williamsport
(717) 322-4714

York
(717) 845-3656

Puerto Rico

Caparra Heights
(809) 765-2285

Cayey
(809) 738-5049

Rhode Island

Cranston
(401) 941-2400

Newport
(401) 846-1213

Providence
(401) 861-4040
(401) 861-5511

South Carolina

Charleston
(803) 722-7273

Greenville
(803) 242-8085

South Dakota

Aberdeen
(605) 225-1010

Brookings
(605) 688-4518

Rapid City
(605) 394-2595

Tennessee

Jackson
(901) 668-1764

Knoxville
(615) 522-7273

Memphis
(901) 528-2161
(901) 528-2247

Nashville
(615) 327-1110

Texas

Abilene
(915) 677-7895

Amarillo
(806) 373-8022

Beaumont
(713) 832-2992

El Paso
(915) 779-1800

Houston
(713) 228-1505
(713) 526-8444
(713) 488-7222

Round Rock
(512) 255-1212

Tyler
(214) 593-2446

Wichita Falls
(817) 723-0821

Alamo
(519) 781-3399

Austin
(512) 472-7273

Dallas
(214) 521-1020

Fort Worth
(817) 336-3355

Killeen
(817) 526-6111

Lubbock
(806) 763-7273

San Antonio
(512) 226-4301

Waco
(817) 752-1113

Utah

Farmington
(801) 867-5581

Ogden
(801) 392-7273

Salt Lake City
(801) 535-5558

Moab
(801) 259-5367

Provo
(801) 373-7393
(801) 375-5111

Vermont

Brattleboro
(802) 254-6954

Burlington
(802) 863-1236

Vermont (Cont.)
Rutland
(802) 775-1000

Virginia
Alexandria
(703) 360-7273
(703) 768-1400

Arlington
(703) 527-4077

Charlottesville
(804) 977-7273
(804) 924-5564

Norfolk
(804) 622-4300

Richmond
(804) 648-9224
(804) 643-0888

Roanoke
(703) 563-0311

Suffolk
(804) 539-0238

Virginia Beach
(804) 463-2000

Washington
Bellingham
(206) 676-1175

Bremerton
(206) 479-3746

Chehalis
(206) 748-6601

Everett
(206) 258-7123

Olympia
(206) 754-2380
(206) 352-2211

Omak
(509) 826-4901

Pullman
(509) 332-4357

Renton
(206) 226-7273

Richland
(509) 943-9104

Seattle
(206) 325-5550
(206) 632-7273
(206) 625-4516
(206) 223-3047

Spokane
(509) 624-7273
(509) 838-4651

Washington (Cont.)

Walla Walla
(509) 529-3377

Tacoma
(206) 627-1135

Yakima
(509) 575-4200

Wenatchee
(509) 663-7446

West Virginia

Charleston
(304) 344-9834

Huntington
(304) 525-7851

Morgantown
(304) 599-6800

Parkersburg
(304) 485-9700

Weirton
(304) 723-5440

Wisconsin

Appleton
(414) 733-8119

Ashland
(715) 682-8114

Green Bay
(414) 468-3553

Jefferson
(414) 674-3105

La Crosse
(608) 784-6419

Madison
(608) 251-5440
(608) 262-4889

Marinette
(715) 735-6621

Milwaukee
(800) 242-9922
(414) 964-7535

Oshkosh
(414) 426-1460

Racine
(414) 633-3233

Stevens Point
(715) 344-4400

Trevor
(414) 658-1717

Wausau
(715) 842-7323

Wyoming

Jackson
(800) 442-6383

Rocksprings
(307) 382-4381

Worland
(307) 347-2674

Rape Crisis Centers in Canada

Alberta
Edmonton
(403) 429-0023

British Columbia
Naniamo
(604) 753-0022

Vancouver
(604) 732-1613

Manitoba
Winnipeg
(204) 774-4525

New Brunswick
Fredericton
(506) 454-0437

Newfoundland
St. John's
(709) 726-1411

Ontario
Guelph
(519) 836-5710

Niagara Falls
(416) 356-9662

Ottawa
(613) 238-6666

Thunder Bay
(807) 344-4502

Ontario (Cont.)
Toronto
(416) 964-8080

Windsor
(519) 253-9667

Quebec
Montreal
(514) 270-8291

Saskatchewan
Regina
(306) 352-0434

Local Rape Crisis Center

_____

_____

_____

Campus Security

_____

_____

_____

Emergency Phone Numbers

_____

_____

_____

_____

_____

_____

Bibliography of Resources

Sources for *Before He Takes You Out*

Recovering from Rape, Linda E. Ledray, Henry Holt & Co., 521 Fifth Ave. New York, NY 10175.

I Never Called it Rape, Robin Warshaw, Harper & Row, Publishers, 10 East 53rd St., New York, NY 10022.

Real Rape, Susan Estrich, Harvard University Press, Cambridge, MA.

I Love You, Let's Work it Out, David Viscott, Simon & Schuster Inc., 1230 Ave. of Americas, New York, NY 10020.

New Life for Men, Joe Vaughn & Ron Klug, Augsburg Publishing House, 426 S. Fifth Street, Box 1209, Minneapolis, MN 55440.

Women's Reality, Anne Wilson Schaef, Harper & Row, Publishers, 10 East 53rd St., New York, NY 10022.

Against Our Will, Susan Brownmiller, Simon & Schuster Inc., 1230 Ave. of Americas, New York, NY 10020.

Surviving Sexual Assault, Congdon & Weed, Inc., 298 Fifth Ave., New York, NY 1001.

The Politics of Rape (The Victim's Perspective), Diana E.H. Russel, Stein and Day Publishers, Scarborough House, Briarcliff Manor, New York, NY 10510.

Choices (Coping Creatively with Personal Change), *The Secret Strength of Depression,* Frederic F. Flach, M.D., J.B. Lippincott Company, Philadelphia & New York.

Turning Fear to Hope, Holly Wagner Green, Thomas Nelson Publishers, Nashville, Camden, New York.

Words That Heal, Douglas Bloch, Pallas Communications, Portland, Oregon.

The Good Girl Syndrome, William Fezler, Ph.D., Eleanor S. Field, Ph.D., Berkley Publishing Group, 200 Madison Avenue, New York, NY 10016.

Your Erroneous Zones, Wayne Dyer, Fitzhenry & Whiteside Ltd., Toronto, Canada.

Rape, Carol V. Horos, Banbury Books, Inc., 37 West Ave., Wayne, PA 19087.

Men on Rape, By Timothy Beneke

The Greatest Miracle in the World, Og Mandino, Bantam Books, 666 Fifth Ave. New York, N.Y. 10103.

Suggested Reading:

In addition to the books listed in the sources, the following books, articles and programs have been recommended by various colleges and universities across the country.

No is Not Enough: Helping Teenagers Avoid Sexual Assault, Adams, Caren & Fay, Jennifer & Loreen-Martin.

Stopping Rape: Successful Survival Strategies, Bart, Pauline & O'Brien, Patricia.

Acquaintance Rape: Alternatives to Fear, Seattle, WA, Bateman, Py.

Her Wits About Her: Self Defense Success Stories by Women, 1987, Caignon, Denise & Gail Groves.

Learning to Live Without Violence: A Handbook for Men, 1985. Sonkin, Daniel & Durphy, Micheal.

So What's It to Me? Information about Sexual Assault for Guys.

> The above literature can be ordered from:
> Ohio State University
> 408 Ohio Union
> 1739 North High St.
> Columbus, Ohio 43210-1392

Passion or Power? The Office of Women's Programs & Services, Division of Student Affairs & Services, University of Cincinnati.

"The Crime Women Never Talk About," Katherine Barrett & Richard Greene, Ladies Home Journal, September 1988.

"Date: Dirty Little Social Secret," Jane Shaw, Woman's Day, 11/5/85.

"The Date Who Rapes," Lifestyle, Newsweek, April 9, 1984.

"Was I Raped?" Elizabeth Kaye, Glamour magazine.

"Dangerous Parties," Paul Keegan, New England Monthly, February 1988.

Friends Raping Friends, Dr. Bernice Sandler, Director of the Project on the Status and Education of Women, Association of American Colleges.

The Crime Victim's Handbook, Nicholas Groth

Coping with Date Rape & Acquaintance Rape, Andrea Parrot, Ph.D. Cornell University, The Rosen Publishing Corp., Inc. 29 E. 21st St. New York, N.Y. 10010.

Audio Visual Aids:

The Acquaintance Rape Tape, Dean's Office, Swarthmore College, Swarthmore, PA 19081.

The Confrontation, Anne Irving, 2434 E. 23rd St., Oakland, CA 94601.

Re-Thinking Rape, Jeanne Le Page, 171 Old La Honda Rd., Woodside, CA 94062.

Speaking Out: Sexual Harassment on Campus, Ruth Hopkins, University of Rochester, Box 617, Rochester, NY 14642.

Surviving Sexual Assault, Rachel Grossman, Joan Sutherland, Congdon and Weed, Inc., New York, 1983.

BEFORE HE TAKES YOU OUT

INDEX:

"Accused, The" (the movie): 20
Affection vs. Sex: 43
Affirmations: 92-95
AIDS, VD: 6, 7, 60, 73
Air horns: 122
Alcohol: 7, 14, 15, 19, 25-38
"Animal House": 29
Anger: 64, 84, 92, 109
Anxiety: 64
Arraignment Hearings: 70
Attitudes (men's): 14, 18, 48
BBB (Better Business Bureau): 113
Bakker, Jim: 87
Beneke, Timothy: 107
Bible, The: 51, 91, 93
Blaming the victim: 35
Bloch, Douglas: 97
Breathing: 59
Bode, Janet: 73
Boston University: 30
Boy next door: 10
Brownmiller, Susan: 45, 83, 106
Bundy, Ted: 20, 30
Choices: 4, 51, 123, 124
Chastity Belts: 10
Communication: 32, 51, 123, 124
Confusion: 34
Control: 46, 100
Criminal prosecution: 70
Crusades: 10
Date rape (definition): 7
Date rape (stages): 13-24
Date rape (triangle): 28
Date rapist: 10
Dating (men & women): 41-43
Denial: 109
Depression: 84, 109
Disbelief: 83, 110
Disorientation: 84
Dormitories: 26
Dyer, Dr. Wayne: 90
Embarrassment: 83
Emerson, Ralph Waldo: 91
Emotions: 63, 64, 81
Equality: 18
Evidence: 76-78
Fault: 81, 127
"Footprints": 96, 97

Fraternities: 25, 26
Fraternity parties: 25, 26
Gang rape: 26, 45
God: 90, 96
"Gone With the Wind": 37, 40
Goodling, Congressman, Bill: 112
Group sex: 26, 45
Guilt: 83, 109
Hahn, Jessica: 87, 88
Helen's story (one woman's story of rape.): 13-23
Holmes, Oliver Wendall: 109
Hospitals: 74, 75
Inner voice: 32, 91
Isolated areas: 19
Jackson, Robert J.: 13
Johnke, Eric: 42
Ledray, Linda: 63, 67
Lincoln, Abraham: 92
Little sisters: 25
"Looking for Mr. Goodbar" (movie): 7
Maclean, Jack: 122
Mace: 120
Mandino, Og: 97
Manipulation: 15, 19
Martial arts: 115
Medical (Evidentiary) exam: 73
Medication: 96
Minimizing (assault): 22
Model mugging: 21, 115-117
National Clearing House on Marital and Date Rape: 107
National Center for Prevention and Control of Rape: 79
Neibuhr, Reinhold: 63
Nightmares: 64
Off campus housing: 26
Over-protection: 110
Parents: 5
Pascal, Blaise: 89
Patience: 111
Paul, Jordan & Margaret: 58
Physical maneuvers: 56, 61, 118
PLAYBOY: 89
Police composite drawing: 68
Police line up: 69
Police report: 67-70
Pornography: 88, 89
Post Trauma Shock: 68
Power: 30
Pregnancy: 78, 79
President George Bush: 1
Pretrial hearing: 70
Priorities: 89
Presecuting Attorney: 69-71
Prosecuting the rapist: 35

R.A.V.E.N. (Rape And Violence End Now): 107
Rape crisis centers: 129-149
Rape (male to male): 103-105
Rape (marital): 107
Rape (traditional view): 2
Rape (statistics): 1, 2, 7-10
Rectin, Andrea: 9
Responsibility (men's): 11, 99
Retriggering: 86
Revenge: 84
Rights (survivor's): 73-80
Rush week: 25
Self control (men): 99-109
Self criticism: 48, 49
Self defense: 115-122
Self punishment: 86, 87, 96
Self worth (men): 41-46
Shame: 64, 83
Shock: 64, 83
Sleeplessness: 64, 93
Socrates: 73
Stranger rapist: 8
Stun guns: 120
Suicide: 86, 87
Suing the rapist: 71
Tear gas: 26, 61, 120, 121
Teasing: 99
Thoughts (changing them): 90-97
Threats of violence: 16, 21
Trump, Donald: 49
Universities: 1, 112-114
Van de Post, Laurens: 25
Vaughn & Klug: 46
Victim Assistance Program: 71, 78
Viscott, Dr. David: 43
Warsaw, Robin: 6, 42, 44, 46, 49
Weapons: 57, 115, 117, 119
Words: 51-56

For more information on date and acquaintance rape, please call Scott Lindquist at (404) 973-1493.

Scott Lindquist is also available for lectures and seminars at your school or university. Mr. Lindquist is an accomplished speaker and has given over 500 seminars to over 250,000 people on crime prevention for hundreds of major corporations and universities. He is one of the most dynamic and successful public speakers in the South. He is able to bridge the gap between student and noted authority. His programs on Date/Acquaintance Rape are both humorous and thoughtfully confrontive. He has spoken to such majpr corporations as: General Electric, A.T.&T.,National Data Corp., Southern Bell, Atlanta Public School System, West Georgia College, Georgia State, University of Georgia, Old Dominion University, Emory University, Morehouse College, Norfolk State, Grady Hospital, 3M Corp., Georgia Power, Texaco, the U. S. Armed Forces and various corporations in Georgia, Alabama, North Carolina, South Carolina, Virginia, Illinois, Arizona, and California.

For information on obtaining the services of Scott Lindquist call: (404) 973-1493, or (404) 973-1440

or write: Scott Lindquist
             c/o Vigal Publishers
             P.O. Box 71452
             Marietta, GA 30067-1452

TEAR GAS ORDER FORM

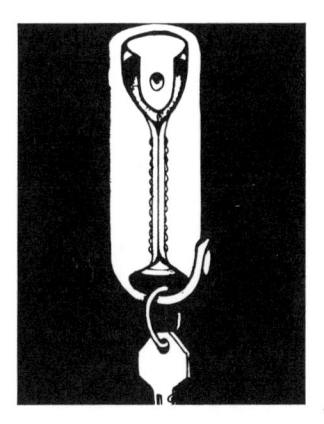

C.S. TEAR GAS has been shown to be an effective non-lethal weapon. This Key Chain tear gas device is connected to your car keys and should be carried to and from your car, work, and home. It can incapacitate the attacker long enough for you to escape. It also contains an ultraviolet dye that marks the assailant for identification purposes. The effects of C.S. Tear Gas will wear off in about 20-30 minutes, and has no side effects. This is harmless but effective! **In Date/Acquaintance Rape situations, where violence is minimal, this can be an excellent deterrent.**

This Key Chain Tear Gas Device comes complete with a key release and small flashlight for shining underneath the car and in the back seat before you enter. This comes from the manufacturer, and is dated for your protection. Tear Gas should be replaced after (1) year.

YES, send me _____ number of tear gas units for my personal protection. The cost of the Key Chain Tear Gas & Light is $17.50 + $2.50 shipping and handling.

Send my tear gas to:
NAME:_____

ADDRESS:_____

_____(ZIP CODE)_____

PHONE: (   ) _____

Send this order to:
V.I.G.A.L.
P.O. Box 71452
Marietta, Georgia 30067-1452
(404) 973-1493 (404) 973-1440

[*Please read disclaimer on back of order form.]

←CUT HERE

* Terms and Conditions of Sale:

The following is in lieu of all warranties, express or implied.
Seller guarantees that each product listed conforms to its standard quality. Seller shall not be liable for any injury, loss or damage, direct or consequential, arising out of the use or the inability to use this product. Before application, user shall determine the suitability of the product for his/her intended use and user assumes all risks and liability whatsoever in connection therewith. Since V.I.G.A.L. has no control over storage, handling, use or application of this product, it must disclaim responsibility for the use or misuse of this product, and all sales are made on condition that V.I.G.A.L., VIGAL Publishers, and the author will not be held liable for any damages resulting from the use of this product.

*PLEASE READ THE ABOVE DISCLAIMER BEFORE ORDERING.

CRIME ALERT AIR HORN ORDER FORM

SCARE THE CRIMINAL AND CALL FOR HELP AT THE SAME TIME!

CRIMINALS HATE LOUD NOISES, AND SO DO MEN WHO ARE ABOUT TO COMMIT DATE/ACQUAINTANCE RAPE. JUST PUSH THE BUTTON AND THE BLAST FROM "CRIME ALERT" WILL STARTLE THE GUY SO THAT YOU CAN ESCAPE. THIS LOUD NOISE CAN BE HEARD FOR UP TO ONE MILE, AND CAN ALSO ALERT NEIGHBORS, ROOMMATES, FRIENDS AND CAMPUS SECURITY THAT YOU NEED HELP!

The CRIME ALERT air horn is a harmless, but effective device that can stop the assault long enough to get away. In Date/Acquaintance Rape situations, where violence is minimal, this can be an excellent deterrent.

The CRIME ALERT air horn does not have a limited shelf life, but because it is a freon product, it should not be stored in the direct sunlight in your automobile. This device can also be used for scaring obscene telephone callers. Be sure to alert your roommates, friends and campus security that when they hear the blast from your CRIME ALERT, to come running... that you are in trouble and need help!

YES, please send me _____ number of CRIME ALERT air horns for my personal protection. The cost of the CRIME ALERT is $14.95 + $2.00 shipping and handling.

Send my CRIME ALERT to:

NAME:_____

ADDRESS:_____

_____(ZIP CODE)_____

PHONE: (   ) _____

Send this order to:
V.I.G.A.L.
P.O. Box 71452
Marietta, Georgia 30067-1452
(404) 973-1493 (404) 973-1440

(The CRIME ALERT is an excellent fund-raiser for college sororities.)

←CUT HERE

THE CIRCLE OF PROTECTION
Audio Tape

IF YOU HAVE BEEN THE VICTIM OF DATE/ACQUAINTANCE RAPE, OR ANY OTHER SERIOUS CRIME, THEN THIS AUDIO TAPE CAN HELP YOU. BY USING THESE SELF HYPNOSIS TECHNIQUES YOU CAN REDUCE THE PARANOIA AND TRAUMA AFTER AN ASSAULT, ALLOWING YOU TO FIND INNER PEACE AND A GREATER SENSE OF PERSONAL SECURITY.

Side One: CIRCLE OF PROTECTION.

This side of the tape is a meditation that creates a circle of protection and peace for you. Inside the circle, you feel calm and safe. You can keep other people's negative statements and actions outside your "Circle of Protec-tion" where they won't affect you. You develop your sense of self control and take back your own power again.

Side Two: FUTURE THINKING.

With this side of the tape you see yourself in the future, "recovered from the trauma of the crime." SEE YOURSELF AS YOU WOULD LIKE TO BE . . . reacting to people, places and things in a healthy and powerful way. THIS TAPE HELPS YOU USE YOUR IMAGINATION AND CREATIVITY TO REBUILD YOUR CONFIDENCE AND SENSE OF SELF WORTH!
THIS WONDERFUL AUDIO TAPE CAN HELP YOU FEEL MORE SECURE AND IN CONTROL OF YOUR LIFE ONCE AGAIN.

YES, please send me _____ number of audio tapes. The CIRCLE OF PROTECTION audio tape is $9.95 + $1.50 shipping and handling.

Please send my tapes to:

NAME:_____

ADDRESS:_____

_____(ZIP CODE)_____

PHONE: (   )_____

Send this order to:
Sydney Magill, C.Ht.
EAST COBB HYPNOSIS CENTER
P.O. BOX 71452
MARIETTA, GEORGIA 30067 - 1452
(404) 973-1493 (404) 973-1440

←CUT HERE

BEFORE HE TAKES YOU OUT
The Safe Dating Guide for the 90's

Book Order Form:

Please send me _____ copies of your book, "BEFORE HE TAKES YOU OUT," The Safe Dating Guide for the 90's. The cost of the book is $9.95 per book, plus $2.50 for shipping and handling (total cost of $12.45 per book). Please allow 3 - 4 weeks for Book Rate. For Air Mail and extra fast delivery, please include an extra $2.55 for Air Mail costs (total cost of $15.00 per book). *Please include local sales tax on books ordered.

BULK DISCOUNTS:
(non-Bookstore Discounts)

1 - 6 Books $9.95 ea. + S&H
7 - 12 Books $9.50 ea. + S&H
13 - 24 Books $9.00 ea. + S&H
25 + Books   Please call for further discounts

Please send books to:

NAME: _____

ADDRESS: _____

_____

ZIP: _____ PHONE: ( ) _____

I am ordering this book for: Please send this form to:
___ Myself
___ My Mother   **VIGAL Publishers**
___ My Daughter   P.O. Box 71452
___ My Sister   MARIETTA, GEORGIA
___ My Grandaughter   30067-1452
___ My Friend   (404) 973-1493
                           (404) 973-1440

←CUT HERE

BEFORE HE TAKES YOU OUT
The Safe Dating Guide for the 90's

Book Order Form:

Please send me _____ copies of your book, "BEFORE HE TAKES YOU OUT," The Safe Dating Guide for the 90's. The cost of the book is $9.95 per book, plus $2.50 for shipping and handling (total cost of $12.45 per book). Please allow 3 - 4 weeks for Book Rate. For Air Mail and extra fast delivery, please include an extra $2.55 for Air Mail costs (total cost of $15.00 per book). *Please include local sales tax on books ordered.

BULK DISCOUNTS:
(non-Bookstore Discounts)

1 - 6 Books $9.95 ea. + S&H
7 - 12 Books $9.50 ea. + S&H
13 - 24 Books $9.00 ea. + S&H
25 + Books   Please call for further discounts

Please send books to:

NAME:_____

ADDRESS:_____

_____

ZIP:_____ PHONE: (   )_____

I am ordering this book for: Please send this form to:
___ Myself
___ My Mother   **VIGAL Publishers**
___ My Daughter   **P.O. Box 71452**
___ My Sister   **MARIETTA, GEORGIA**
___ My Grandaughter   **30067-1452**
___ My Friend   **(404) 973-1493**
                                 (404) 973-1440

←CUT HERE

BEFORE HE TAKES YOU OUT
The Safe Dating Guide for the 90's

Book Order Form:

Please send me _____ copies of your book, "BEFORE HE TAKES YOU OUT," The Safe Dating Guide for the 90's. The cost of the book is $9.95 per book, plus $2.50 for shipping and handling (total cost of $12.45 per book). Please allow 3 - 4 weeks for Book Rate. For Air Mail and extra fast delivery, please include an extra $2.55 for Air Mail costs (total cost of $15.00 per book). *Please include local sales tax on books ordered.

BULK DISCOUNTS:
(non-Bookstore Discounts)

1 - 6 Books $9.95 ea. + S&H
7 - 12 Books $9.50 ea. + S&H
13 - 24 Books $9.00 ea. + S&H
25 + Books   Please call for further discounts

Please send books to:

NAME: _____

ADDRESS: _____

_____

ZIP: _____ PHONE: ( ) _____

I am ordering this book for: Please send this form to:
___ Myself
___ My Mother   **VIGAL Publishers**
___ My Daughter   **P.O. Box 71452**
___ My Sister   **MARIETTA, GEORGIA**
___ My Grandaughter   **30067-1452**
___ My Friend   **(404) 973-1493**
                                (404) 973-1440

←CUT HERE

BEFORE HE TAKES YOU OUT
– EMERGENCY CARD –

The emergency card on this page will help you to remember the most vital information you may need in the event of a potentially dangerous situation. Fold this card and cut along the dotted line. Place inside your wallet or purse in an easily accessible place.

CUT

1. Is he emotionally abusing you?
2. Is he making decisions for you?
3. Is he talking negatively about women?
4. Is he irrationally jealous?
5. Is he using drugs/alcohol?
6. Is he trying to get you intoxicated?
7. Is he berating you for not getting drunk/high with him?
8. Is he insisting on paying for you?
9. Is he intimidating you by getting too close?
10. Is he touching you against your will?
11. Is he insisting on taking you away from other people?
12. Do you feel uncomfortable with him?
13. What is your "inner voice" telling you to do?

FOLD

IF IT HAPPENS TO YOU . . .

1. GET TO SAFETY.
2. DON'T WASH, CHANGE OR URINATE.
3. REPORT THE CRIME (where it happened).
4. GET A MEDICAL EXAM.
5. CALL A SUPPORTIVE FRIEND.
6. CALL RAPE CRISIS CENTER.
7. DON'T BE ALONE (Have a friend stay over).
8. FIND A SUPPORT GROUP.
9. DON'T MINIMIZE WHAT HAPPENED.
10. REMEMBER, IT'S NOT YOUR FAULT.

CUT   CUT

FOLD

Campus Security: Phone _____
Police: Phone _____
Address: _____
Rape Crisis Center: Phone _____
Friend/Roommate: Phone _____
Your Doctor: Phone _____
Parents: Phone _____
Address: _____
_____

CUT

**SAFE DATING
EMERGENCY CARD**

**SAFE DATING
EMERGENCY CARD**

**SAFE DATING
EMERGENCY CARD**